Firepower Books

THE TRUTH ABOUT WINTER

Dixie Gillaspie

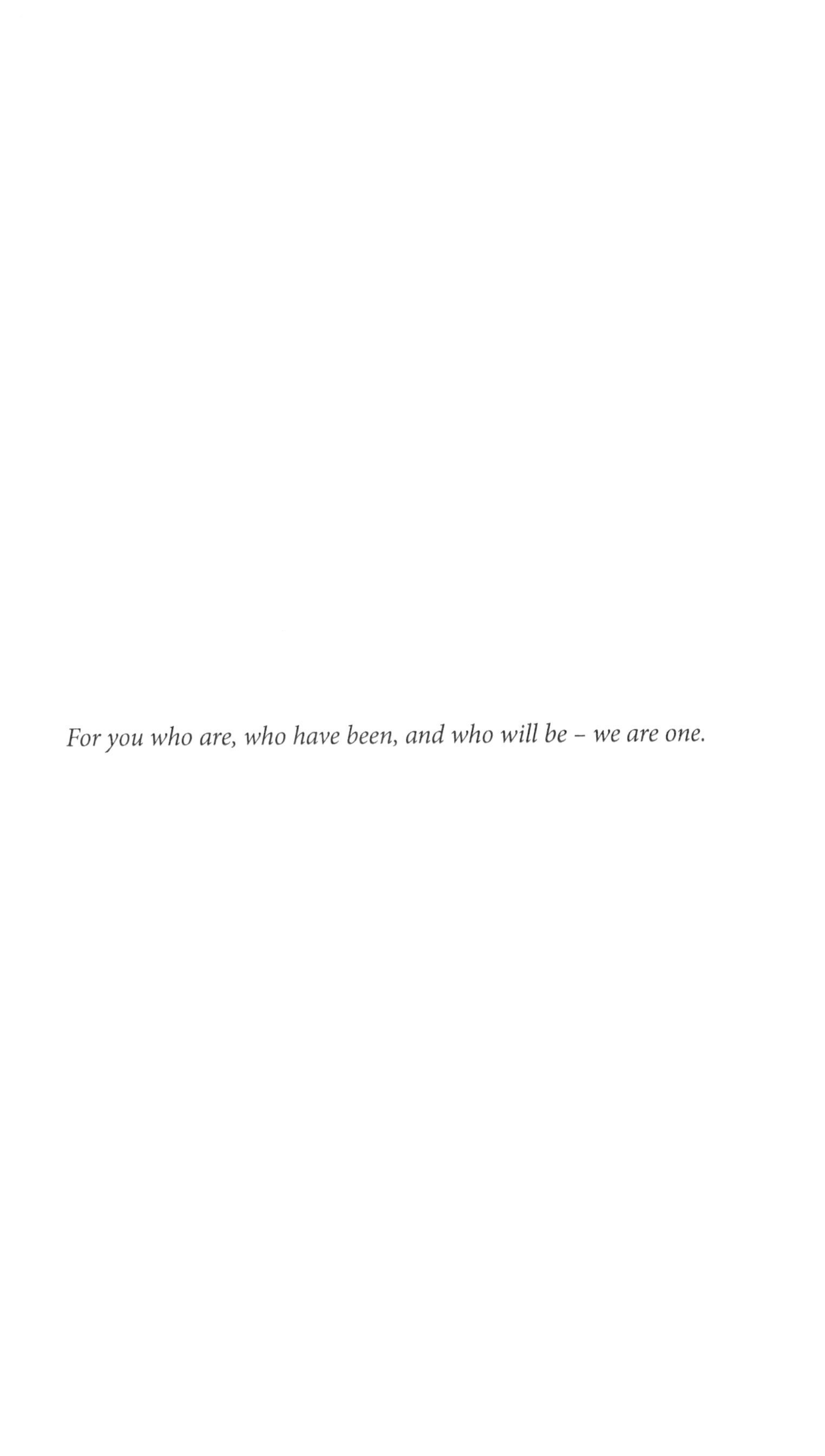

For you who are, who have been, and who will be – we are one.

CONTENTS

DISCLAIMER

This book is a work of fiction, but of course I've blended in some events, locales, and conversations from my memories of them. Most characters and places have had their names changed or were created from whole cloth. I've made no attempt to create accurate accounts of events, but rather told the story as it seemed to me at the time or as it could have been in a parallel universe and nothing in this story is presented as or intended to be taken as fact.

About the themes in this book I feel it is only kind and appropriate to add a TRIGGER WARNING. As a person who has experienced both the traumas described here and the triggers that are a common result of those experiences I know it can be difficult to navigate stories dealing with physical violence, rape, and emotional abuse. All of those themes appear in this book because they were part of my life and I want you to know that whatever you feel reading those pages is appropriate and true for you, just as the feelings I had for many years of my life were appropriate and true for me. I no longer have triggered reactions to these themes, and this book is a fictionalized account of how I moved through trauma into a life where those experiences have no power to harm me. It is written as a gift of love to all, but especially to those who are still reliving their trauma and wish to live in their power. So remember, you can choose to read this, to lay it aside, to come back to it when it feels right, but most of all, you have the power to choose your own truth and your own life.

Dixie Gillaspie
November, 2022

AUTHOR'S NOTE

Every story has three levels of truth: The truth of what actually happened. The truth of what we remember and *believe* has happened. And the truth we choose, the one that will transform us when we step into our power and own the story of what happened.

It is rare that we have absolute truth about what actually happened. Our brains are wired to lie to us, to filter and delete, to distort our perception and memory to align with patterns set before we were fully formed. Our minds are conditioned to attach more meaning to some things than others, to find meaning where there is none, and to fail to notice nuances of meaning where they exist.

Even in an age where there are cameras in every purse and pocket, where recordings of events are dished up indiscriminately as news, entertainment, and education, we know that even recorded images do not capture the truth, and what is captured can easily be manipulated to appear to be what it was not. So what we see, and what we're programmed to remember and believe is seldom, if ever, the truth of actual events, let alone the truth of the meaning of those events.

The power of story, historical or fictional, is less in remembering what happened, or reconciling ourselves to what we believe happened, and more in choosing how we will be transformed by the happenings. To that end, in the following story, I have liberally woven my memories with fictional creations to share the truth of my own choices and my own transformation.

Here in this place and on these pages, I have consecrated *my* truths. Written and unwritten, spoken and unspoken, known and unknown. They are here in the lines and between the lines for you to discover, and in discovering, to learn, not my truths, but a way to choose your own.

It is my desire that you take what I have shared – not as fact or prescription – but as inspiration for you to step into your own power, to make your own choices, and create your own transformations.

Here, today, I step fully into the power of my own truth. Irrevocably and eternally. May you choose to do the same.

MARCH

Wind.

Out here on the Kansas prairie it's a living thing.

Eyes closed tight, I lift my face and let it tear at my hair. Its wild fingers tug long strands away from my skull, lift the collar of my blouse, and bring tears to my eyes.

Alone on the roof of the crude stone castle, I rest my hands behind me on the top of the parapet wall, and let the sun warm my back. Both sun and wind feel nearly solid.

I turn to face the slowly sinking ball of fire, the light lying heavy like a compress against my skull, my cheekbones, my collarbone. In the watery haze of tear-blind vision I see the ground below diving away down the rocky hill. Through that misty lens I see myself falling – not leaping, not cartwheeling – just plummeting like a bird who, feeling the limb beneath her beginning to crack, has let go but forgotten how to open her wings.

I haven't really left the rooftop, but my consciousness feels more one with the body fast approaching the ground than it does with the feet firmly planted on concrete, the hands gripping the top of the barrier that is all that stands between the solid me and the me that vanishes a split second before the body thuds to the rocks below.

I've had these visions before, of my body moving away from safety, away from wholeness, away from life. There've been times when it was more than a vision, when I came into myself to find that my material body had followed the vision to perch on the outside edge of a balcony looking out from some 20 stories high over a Maui shoreline or to step confidently and surely into the spot where a bus was about to pull up for its designated stop.

The therapist, when my husband, Tom, insisted I see one, had nodded in a way I supposed she thought would make her appear experienced, jaded even for all of her less than 30 years of life, and in a voice meant to sound wise or at least authoritative said something like, "I'd like for you to see our psychiatrist, you exhibit the classic symptoms of …" But the … ended with the word "victim" which wasn't me, so I discounted everything she said before or after.

I did see "their" psychiatrist. I don't remember anything he said, only that the prescription he wrote was for something that caused me to have such vivid, horrid dreams that I left off taking it and didn't go back to see what else he might have to say.

Since then the visions, both sleeping and waking, are more rare and less vivid. But I know they're there, playing in the background. I've just learned not to tune into the wavelength they're playing on. I suppose that the companionship of sun and wind and the vastness of the unpeopled fields around me simply lulled me into widening my senses, lowering my barriers, seeing what might be and, if I'm speaking my truest thoughts, what might not be such a bad thing in the end.

Looking across the fields before me, I realize they aren't completely unpeopled, not any more. Far off, I see a horse and rider approaching the Kansas castle. I watch them idly, shielding my eyes against the light, until a bend in their course hides them from view.

They call this place Coronado Heights. A high point in a land that appears to be flat, except those times of year when the swell of tasseled corn towers over neighboring wheat.

In truth, Kansas is like the sea that once covered its prairies, it rolls and undulates. Even the Flint Hills, showing striated layers where they have been bisected for the roads to cut through, look like waves reaching toward a shore. The rutted path that climbs to reach the flat top of this erosional hill threads through layers of red and grey before becoming golden sandstone.

It is said that Coronado used this point as a lookout on his 1541 venture, searching for the mythical kingdom of Quivira. The rough Spanish style mock-fortress was built nearly 400 years later on funding from the Works Progress Administration by men returning from World War I. Victorious survivors who came back to a country exploding with industry and a surfeit of live bodies to fill the jobs that still required human hands.

Waiting for the galloping pair to come into view again, I consider the grid of fields and roads spread below me, picturing the landscape as it might have looked in 1932. Not the neat Kansas countryside of my childhood memories, but fields riddled with rocks and roughly tilled, often as not, by horse drawn cultivators.

Then would have come the hordes of unemployed and the New Deal Agency. Between one war and the next, fields were cleared, walls were built, and the fanciful stone castle, firepits, tables, and benches were left as a place for families to picnic, for teens to use as a not-so-secret lovers' haven, and for the likes of me to stand – resigning dead dreams to the sun and wind.

I wonder about the men who bent to the earth to remove each stone, who carried them here and fitted them to a purpose that was surely trivial to minds honed by days, weeks, even years of life and freedom held in the balance. What would they have thought of the work they were given to do?

How would it shape a person, to look at death every day? To sleep with him nestled close like a malicious kitten, and wake to find him grown into a ravaging lion? To see him claim both friend and foe? And finally, to have him take his claws out of your spine and swat you dismissively home, only to find that home had precious little to offer except labor in the Kansas sun, building a toy castle on a miniature mountain.

It makes me feel a little less bitter, to believe that people who once stood where I now stand thought darker thoughts than I now think. To know that, if their dreams were as sweet as any I have dreamed, at least I can be grateful that mine were not torn from me by war. If my dreams are dead, at least thousands did not die with them.

I can hear the horse's hooves, thudding over the so-called virgin prairie. Nothing like as unmolested as it was when Coronado surveyed the Smokey Valley below, but still pridefully billed as "virgin" on the Lindsborg, Kansas websites. Horse and rider are out of sight as they approach the bottom of the hill. I hear the hoof beats slow as they pick their way up the steep, winding path.

I rest my elbows on the parapet wall, put my chin in my hands, and watch for them to top the rise. They do, in a burst of energy and clatter of hooves, the horse shaking a golden head, pale mane backlit by the dying sun.

The rider sits straight, but at ease, hands loose on the reins, dark hair streaming in the same wind that tugs at my own strands. Perched bareback on the big horse, she looks tiny, almost doll-like. Something in her bearing puts me in the mind of an ancient warrior. She sits the horse like an Amazon straight out of myth, only in miniature.

As the duo comes closer, I realize the smallness isn't an illusion of distance and angle, the rider is only a child. Just as I register her youthful features, she raises a hand to me, more a salute than a wave, and urges her mount to the trail that winds down the gentle slope of the south side of the hill. I shield my eyes with my hand again, squinting to keep them in view as they move smoothly over the waving prairie grasses and away from my fortress made of wind, and sun, and stone.

I watch them go, expecting them to fade into nothing, become the vapor of imagination I feel certain that they are, no more real than the vision of my own body almost meeting the stony hilltop where the horse and rider had just been.

The opening lines of a poem come to me, something I'd written driving through the Flint Hills just as they revealed their pre-spring dress.

Out of the hollows where the earth grows thin
Between the hills all swathed in gold and green
I watched the band of faerie riders come…

And there it ended. "Died aborning" as the old wives would say. Like so many things had for me of late. Died aborning.

The old ache hits me, of words unsaid, lines unwritten, truths glimpsed but ungleaned and irretrievable. I look into the spaces of me where magic used to live and all I see are deadlines and rows of facts and figures. There's something about these almost-flat hills of Kansas that made me feel almost-creative. But not quite.

The sun is not so warm on my back now, and the wind has an edge. I run my hands over the rough stones topping the parapet wall before crossing to the steep, spiraling staircase that descends into the lower room with its fireplace and picnic tables. Maybe next time I'll bring a snack. Maybe not.

I drive carefully down the rocky track to the country highway. The road curves around the edge of the little Swedish town of Lindsborg, then carves a straight line south, to McPherson, where I will spend the evening readying my notes for the workshop I'll be conducting tomorrow and trying to fix the vision of my warrior child and her horse in my memory. Finding, somehow, it was already there.

She is baby-plump and pale sun-golden, the little one sitting on the blanket on the ground. Almost-white ringlets tipped with gilt might have been neatly brushed when the day began, but now show distinct signs of having been ruffled by her own baby fingers, by adult's doting palms, and by the light and capricious breeze that stirs the old fashioned sweet peas rioting over a trellis nearby.

"Hello, sweet baby," says the dreaming me. She doesn't hear.

The warrior child moves so softly and surely I don't hear her footfalls as she glides out from behind the laden trellis. She holds a few choice blossoms – sweet peas and sweet williams, and a single yellow rose. Her flame-red cotton sundress skims her almost woman's body, widening into a full skirt around her knees. When she kneels in front of the baby, the folds make a sunset pool on the sky-blue blanket. The baby waves her little fists, opening them into reaching fingers, wanting the pretty posies.

They are both laughing, the carefree baby and the self-contained child, and the sun catches at the pale gold of the baby and the dark gold of the child, and I think, in the fanciful way a dreamer does, that the sun is laughing too.

The baby's fingers reach the little bouquet and brush the satin tip of the half-opened rose. From its center rises a bee. I hold my breath.

The bee buzzes in indignation at being disturbed. The child does not blink, but the baby's eyes widen as she tries to follow the erratic path of the bee, nearly crossing as it zips toward her and lands on a fold of delicate skin just behind her ear. I brace myself for her scream.

I try to dream the baby into stillness. Try to dream the bee into flight. Try to dream myself awake before the bee does what bees are predisposed to do when they are disoriented and land on things that move unexpectedly.

The baby screams. And what a scream it is. If the bee was indignant, the baby is *outraged*. That *hurt!* That tiny, pretty humming thing *hurt* her! The unjustness offends her baby understanding as completely as the sudden pain offends her tender skin.

The child kneels, unperturbed. The baby's fists wave in rage, her face already mottled and wet with tears. Rooted in my dreamscape, I reach out my arms, aching to hold and comfort the little one. Why doesn't that child go for help if she is not strong enough to lift the crying baby? She looks to be about twelve or thirteen, plenty old enough to know what to do. Slender though she is, the sun browned arms show the curve of muscle.

"Pick up that baby and get her inside!" I am silent-sleeping-observer, still I try to make her hear me.

The child does not obey, of course. She does put the posies aside and reaches out her hands to lay them over the baby's waving fists.

I hear running footsteps moving toward our little scene. Thank heavens, adults. Surely someone will come get the baby and put something soothing on that nasty sting. I suspect the poor dear is more scared than hurt, and needs comfort more than medical attention, but bee stings can be nasty business.

"Little One," I hear the child's voice crooning, surprisingly deep and throaty for one so young. "The bee was only looking for pollen, she intended no harm. Breathe, Little One, just breathe."

"Some comfort that is," I murmur in my sleep. "So the bee didn't *mean* to hurt her. Like a baby understands that. She doesn't care about that bee, she's scared. She needs to be held. Now!"

The adults are on the scene, two of them. Indistinct woman figures moving through my dream as supporting roles only, no features required. They both kneel on the blanket, reaching for the baby. One swoops her up, not glancing at the child, and trots toward the house I see in the corner of my mind's eye. The other touches the abandoned flowers with a puzzled air before trotting after the first, the baby's screams fading to hiccupping sobs.

"What an odd dream," my thinking self whispers to my dreaming self. "The phone should ring soon, wakeup call at 6:30. The baby's fine, you have a big day ahead. You should wake up now."

But the dreamer goes on dreaming, floating in a bodiless state.

Captive to the dream, I follow the women characters as they carry the little one into the house. I sense the child following behind as well, but I don't turn to look. Something is not right with that one, I think. Who could just sit calmly when a baby is hurting and scared like that?

In fact, if that bee was so disturbed, surely it had buzzed, even a little, surely she should have known the peril that rose harbored? Of course, it hadn't been her peril, the bee hadn't stung her, had it? Only the unsuspecting baby who didn't know to just be still and let the bee fly away without causing any harm.

I'm screaming at her now, the slim, straight figure in the flame-red dress. "WHAT WERE YOU THINKING?" My voice cracks with emotion, my throat tight in my sleep, though I know I produce no sound.

She follows me without flinching.

The women figures reach the house, a country cottage type of place that feels vaguely familiar. My dream supplies no details except the screen door already closing behind them. I open it. Silly thing to do since the dreaming me could pass right through it, but even in our dreamscapes we maintain some sense of normalcy I suppose. Out of habit, I hold it for the child. She nods, perhaps mocking me for the gesture. We go inside together.

The woman has placed the baby on a Formica-topped kitchen table. I gasp to see her face now. What I had taken for mottling from the effort of screaming is obviously something far more threatening. They have stripped her of all but her cotton diaper. The white dress she had been wearing lies discarded over the back of a chair. Angry welts have formed on skin that had been pale gold only minutes before, and I can see streaks of red where the swelling cannot be contained by the little body.

Tears leap to my eyes. I feel them on my cheeks in both my dreaming state and my sleeping wakefulness. One of the woman figures is spreading a white paste over the baby's face and shoulders, the other holds the receiver of a corded phone and is talking rapidly, the panic rippling in her voice tones, agitation apparent in every line of her stance.

The child moves around me to hoist herself up on the edge of the table near the baby's head. Neither of the woman figures acknowledge her in any way. She perches there, on the edge of the table, close enough that the top of the baby's head is almost in her lap. She lays a hand gently on the gilt curls, probably the only place she could touch that isn't in agony.

I hear her, even though she whispers, "You're having a reaction, Little One. That's all. This is just your reaction, and you can choose."

The baby's eyes open, a startling aqua blue against the blotched red face. She looks up, right into the eyes of the calm child above her, and they both smile.

Next morning I'm tired and cranky. My hair wants to curl, a sure sign of wet weather on the way. My eyes have plum-colored circles under them that no amount of makeup will cover completely.

Self-pity overwhelms me. Rain would be my absolutely last straw. I have to drive to the airport in Wichita tomorrow, an hour of what will likely be wet roads, and neither my mood nor my appearance is going to be improved by another day of "yeah-but-that-won't-work-for-us-it's-hard-why-do-we-have-to-do-it-that-way" whining from a staff that has no clue how lucky they are to work for a guy who actually cares what they think.

The day passes. Most days will do that. By six o'clock I'm feeling like a guest on the Jerry Springer show; everything I say is ridiculed, turned into drama, then dismissed at the end of the segment.

I'm the consultant, I *should* be able to command more respect from this staff. Goodness knows they're happy enough to collect the profit sharing bonuses that they're drawing as a result of the growth of the business. Not that they're willing to connect that payout with the changes I've put in place, I'm just the necessary-evil-means-to-an-end who flies in every month to torture them into doing what they're paid to do in the first place. I wallow in this bitter brew while I grab the latest production reports off the printer and close down the computer.

Waiting for the computer to go through its closing routine, I lean back and close my eyes. Last night's dream replays on the backs of my eyelids. It wasn't really a nightmare, not like the ones I used to have over and over when I was younger. Yet, I feel dread at the thought that I might visit that strangely familiar scene again.

Tonight will be a change from the casual debrief over dinner that I usually do with this client. He and his wife have a guest this evening, and I've been asked to join them, so no business talk. That will be a respite, maybe they won't notice if I doze off while they carry on about the crops and the latest rumors of layoffs at the local oil refinery.

Standing in the parking lot, I'm glad that there are only a few cars left. I've completely forgotten which rental I have this week. The dark blue Chrysler or the little red Chevy? No, the red car was in Tulsa last week, the blue sedan winks at me as I press the unlock button on the key fob.

Driving through small town streets toward my client's gracious home, I'm reminded of my hometown. Or what *was* my hometown before I left it forever. I stop at a red light, the two older ladies crossing the street wave cheerily at me without even looking closely enough to realize that they don't know me at all. They know everyone, what are the chances that I am an exception to that rule?

I'm struck by a throat-clenching burst of homesickness. That memory-place isn't home anymore, and never will be again. But I can't really say where I left home behind, or where I will go when I go "home."

While I sit looking behind my eyes for something I never want to find, the light changes. Small town folk may not have the city habit of gunning away from green lights, but they won't sit and wait forever. The honk isn't a blare, but the gentle "beep" still startles me into motion.

Dinner is pleasant. Milt and Toni introduce me as their "lifesaver," and that lifts my spirits a bit. I know they sincerely value the expertise and effort I dedicate to their business, and the trials we are experiencing now are going to be resolved with some staffing changes soon. Feeling a little less like the outsider at the table, I tune into the conversation.

Their guest is a burly rancher who was a neighbor before taking over his parents' ranch. He goes by "Bud" – no telling what his given name might have been. It's my experience that every town in rural America has to have at least one "Bud."

This Bud is a real character. He would be a stereotype of Americana except for the twinkle of subtle intelligence in his shrewd, direct gaze, and the grace with which he carries his large frame. No bumbling good ole boy here. He asks about me, where do I live, and then do I really come all the way from St. Louis out to the middle of Kansas every month just to keep Milt in line?

We laugh about the impossibility of *anyone* keeping Milt in line. Toni and I together can keep him from hanging himself most days, I tell Bud. But some days we just leave him to his own devises and hope we can pick up the debris later. Milt laughs too. He knows his tendency to speak first, think later, is a trial to both Toni and me. He also knows that his transparent honesty is one of the reasons we love him, each in our own way.

I've been coming here to work with Milt in his business for over seven years. We've had tremendous success together, the staff issues we're experiencing now really are unusual and, we hope, temporary. Having Bud tell me that he's been looking forward to meeting me after hearing Milt and Toni talk about how they enjoy having me work with them each month sets my bruised ego very nearly to rights again.

"So little lady," Bud is saying to me, "I understand you're quite the horsewoman."

I'm startled. Horses have always been one of my loves. I still can't drive by a pasture with even a single horse without slowing. But I don't know how he got the impression I have any expertise.

"I wouldn't say that, Bud. I don't know much *about* riding really. I had horses, and I rode them, but no one ever taught me anything. I'd make a poor horsewoman by your standards, I'll bet."

He eyes me with a wry smile. "Oh, I don't think being a horsewoman has a thing to do with ridin' 'em," he says slowly. "I think it has a lot more to do with knowin' 'em."

I grin back at him, he's just given me a status I'd always craved and never thought I'd earned. "Then I guess I qualify," I reply. "I don't know much about riding, actually I don't know much *about* horses. But I do know horses, if that makes any sense."

"Makes a lot of sense. Tell me about your favorite horse."

"I don't know if I could pick one favorite," I begin. He's already nodding, I haven't surprised him with that one. "My first horse wasn't a horse. She was only a pony, a Shetland mare who'd never been broke to ride. She'd been used in pulling contests and she was terribly skittish. But her name was Trixie and it rhymed with Dixie, and I thought she was just destined to be mine."

I go on, telling him about the challenges of getting that little bay pony to tolerate me, let alone to trust me. The hundreds, maybe thousands of times I fought to get a bridle on her, only to get on and be thrown off, get back on and be thrown off again. I watch the amusement on his creased face when I share the joy I felt the first time Trixie came to me and reached out her nose to touch the bit I held warming in my hand, the thrill of slipping the head stall over her ears and having her stand, patient but eager, while I lofted myself onto her back.

"The *best* horse I ever got to ride," I'm feeling euphoric, effects of the troubled night forgotten, "was on a ranch that was close to our house. It was owned by a big corporation out of Wichita, and they also bred Quarters for the tracks down in Hot Springs." I know he'll get the lingo, that I am talking about Quarter Horses – bred to race on quarter-mile tracks like the ones that Hot Springs, Arkansas is famous for.

With a quirk of a smile he lets me know he gets it.

"They brought their mares to the ranch to foal," I explain. "There was always a window of time when they could be ridden but not raced. Since my parents were friends with the ranch foreman, and I rode down there pretty often, they let me ride them."

Now I am completely transported. Back to the summer I turned seventeen. My father was gone a lot, my mother was weary of fighting my wild child ways, and I was free to run the countryside like a native spirit. I was up early, never my wont, but worth it to have the rest of the day to myself, finished my chores and headed for the ranch. I'd sit dreaming on the top rail of a fence, pick blackberries for a late breakfast, swim in the shale-bottomed pond, and ride.

The ranch offered many choices of mounts and, if they weren't being used to cut cattle, I was welcome to saddle any of them. Gentle, solid Bob, sure of foot and deep of heart – we could go all day then come back to the pasture where I'd pull off his tack and let him follow me into the pond. He'd nose at the flashing minnows, and I'd use his broad back as a diving board.

Or there was Misty, black as night, temperamental as a summer storm. She could turn on a dime and, if she was in the mood, she'd take me jumping over dry creek beds and flying up and down the pasture ridges, whooping with the dangerous thrill of what we might discover over the next rise.

But it was Ginger who took my breath away. She was well-named; her coat was exactly the color of the ginger I pulled from the cabinet when I made spice cookies. I never knew if she took any purses on the tracks in Arkansas, but she stole my heart with her haughty airs, flowing mane, and fiery spirit. She would race anything that moved.

Forgetting how I had dreaded this evening, I tell Bud about that summer with Ginger. I didn't have racing tack, I tell him. The ranch only had the heavier Western gear, and I'd never ridden with anything else, except bareback.

"So I couldn't really get up on her withers, you know." I'm on a rave now. "And even then I was heavier than a jockey, about 125 and solid muscle. But she could still just fly! One time we were coming back to the ranch on a dirt road and a pickup came up behind us. I reined her over, but all she knew was there was something gaining on her and that wouldn't do. I couldn't hold her – don't know that I tried really hard –we raced that truck all the way to the stables."

We're all laughing, sharing the picture of me, not-quite-seventeen, perched up on the big race horse, rising above the saddle horn to move as high on her withers as I could, hair flying and a grin that took over all of my face. With a start I see another figure in the scene my mind's eye is recreating. The same slight figure in flame red cotton I'd seen out on the prairie and again in my dream. Up on the big horse. I can't place the breed. Fast and agile, with a feathery mane and tail and a pale gold dappled coat.

I know I am distracting my mind with this detail to avoid watching the girl, not riding upright at a canter now, but lying almost flat against her mount's neck and holding close to Ginger and me as we race like a lightning bolt down the dirt road in my memory.

I bring myself back to the table, the cozy dining room with three smiling faces just finishing expressions of delight and mirth.

"I guess I get a little carried away," I admit sheepishly, trying not to betray my unease at finding that memory invaded by yet another encounter with my odd prairie vision. "Let me get those dishes, Toni, you guys have catching up to do."

I drive back to the hotel with the tiredness settling around my shoulders again. Tonight might require another cup of coffee, I think, remembering the reports I'd pulled off the printer but hadn't touched. Tomorrow will be easier, but still intense. Knowing there is a staffing crisis brewing, we'd decided to start interviewing for potential team members. So I'll spend the day conducting interviews then driving to Wichita to turn in the rental and catch a flight home. Not a flight I want to miss, it's the last non-stop to St. Louis; missing it means rerouting through Dallas with a long layover.

In the shower I stand under the hot water longer than necessary to get clean and not long enough to dissolve the knots in my shoulders. I tell myself those reports can wait until after I get home tomorrow night. I can even review them on the plane. Milt and I aren't going to have time to talk about them before I leave anyway.

Sitting on the bed, I pull out the little red book that has traveled everywhere with me since it fell into my hands when I was fourteen. When I am home, it stays on my bedside table. When I travel, it goes in my carryon bag.

It's a hardcover book, but someone has replaced the original with a wrapping of red fabric. Picked out on the cover in gold thread is a single word; "Truths." Below are flaws in the fabric where stitches have been pulled from the cloth. I've never been able to connect those dots to form a word or a picture.

After searching bookstores and, as it became a primary research medium, the internet, and never finding a reference to any of the phrases that cover its pages, I'd decided it must have been something that someone self-published for their own use and inspiration. The cloth cover clearly isn't original to the book, but I treasure it the way it is and have never tried to remove it to see what lies beneath.

It isn't a story book, more of a devotional or journal. Each page boasts only a single quote in a flowery typeface with blank lines below, presumably to allow the reader to append their own thoughts.

Another book, one that I discovered about the time that this little red volume came into my hands, said that you can use any book, or even a newspaper, to find answers to a dilemma just by closing your eyes, holding the problem in your mind, and reading the first thing your eyes settle on when you open them.

That has become a practice for me, and I try it now, letting the book fall open in my hands. The flowery script on the left side reminds me:

There is a reason dreams are conceived while sleeping. That is the only time the rational mind can't sneak in and abort them before they hatch.

Followed, on the next page, by;

Are you dreaming true dreams? Or only living out a fantasy?

I can't see how that answers my problem of being bone-deep weary and frustrated into unreasonableness. Nor do I see how it speaks to my recurring vision of the horse and warrior child I'd seen from the prairie fortress yesterday. True dreams, or fantasy? Of course she's a fantasy! But what is she to me?

I decide that tonight sleep is more likely to offer perspective than my little red book. I click off the light, put my head on the mushy hotel pillow and close my eyes.

More dreams play on the screen of my eyelids like a series of movie trailers. Intense action and frozen vignettes interspersed.

Blonde pigtails. Calico print dress. Small hands gripping the long, curved horns of a pale cream nanny goat, the goat's four legs planted as firmly as the four-year-old's two sturdy brown ones. So perfectly matched are they that neither moves.

A cluster of boys surrounds a galvanized washbasin. The boys lean in, there's a pathetic mewl, then nothing. She bursts on the scene like a storm cloud, wielding a baseball bat, sunlight glinting off long bronzed braids, fury edging her voice. The boys flee, the kitten forgotten. She drops the bat, scoops up the bedraggled baby and wraps it in her skirt, cooing like an outraged dove.

By the time the phone jangles with my wakeup call, I've forgotten most of the scenes. I remember enough to realize they aren't dreams exactly, but snippets of memory, gone unvisited for years. I wonder if my dream of the night before last is also a memory. If that pale golden baby girl had been me, then who is the dark gold child with somber eyes and a warrior's bearing?

My subconscious must be drawing on some memory, some reflection of events of my own childhood, but I sure can't place any of them now. I don't *remember* having an imaginary friend. Characters in books were my constant companions; I knew Heidi and Jo and the Boxcar Children better than I knew my own siblings, grown and gone to start lives of their own before I was old enough to remember. The warrior child is certainly familiar to me, but I'm pretty sure she isn't a character in a book, nor do I believe that she's ever before been part of my dreams or visions. Not the ones I've had while sleeping, and certainly not the ones I've had while I was awake.

Timeliness has never been my forte. This morning though, I have time to pack and throw my suitcase in the trunk, check out of the hotel, and hit a fast food drive-thru for coffee and a breakfast sandwich. The girl's presence is so tangible in the car with me that I consider offering her some of my hash browns. I don't need the calories, and she could use some extra meat on her bones. I swallow the last bite, turn into the office parking lot, and make it to the door only three minutes late instead of my usual five or even ten.

Her presence paces me to the desk. "Maybe she's good at employee selection," I joke to myself. "Pick us a good one," I say to her silently. Never hurts to cover all the bases.

My flight lands on time. Tom is there to pick me up, but he's used to me arriving weary and silent, so he doesn't see anything amiss when I hug him briefly before giving him my suitcase to hoist into the trunk, toss my computer case and purse on the back seat, then slide gratefully into the car without another word. Headed home. Sleeping in my own bed tonight.

I hadn't reviewed those reports, had instead pulled out my little red book and thumbed through the pages as the plane filled with people as anxious as I to get to St. Louis.

Life is not precious because we can lose it, but precious because we can choose it.

I'd heard again the words from my dream, "This is just your reaction, and you can choose." Not knowing what to think of that, not really wanting to think of that, I had gazed out the window, watching the earth fall away, enjoying the change in perspective as the details became less and less plain. Once we were in the cloud cover, I had turned to the red book again.

I'd stroked its fabric covering and remembered finding it, buried in a box of books that my parents picked up at an estate sale. That alone was a little odd because I had personally selected the books in that box. Crouched underneath one of the long tables, laden with remnants of a life now for sale to the highest bidder, I'd rummaged through the boxes of books, sorting them – not by value since I knew nothing of antique books – but according to my instincts and interests.

Books that I wanted went into one or two boxes, books I didn't want went into the rest. I'd been doing this since I could read, estate sale after estate sale. I'd tug on my mother's sleeve, "Get that one, Mom," I'd whisper when my special boxes were being carried to the auctioneer. "There are books I want in that one, please?"

I wasn't accustomed to getting everything I asked for, not by any means, but books were one area where my mother indulged me. My father was frustrated by my obsession with "story books," an obsession that was fed and fostered by a mother who read to me for hours on end until I learned to recognize words before I was old enough for kindergarten. So if the box didn't go for too much money, it came to me, brimming with people I hadn't met, words I didn't know, and worlds I hadn't yet discovered. I devoured them and, if I liked them, I read them again and again.

I'm sure *I* didn't put that little red book in the middle of a stack of books in one of my special boxes. That's where I found it though – not placed casually on top by some other curious sorter, but in the middle of the heap, between an old age-spotted copy of Louisa May Alcott's *Rose in Bloom* and a volume of poetry from some college course I'd never take.

Sitting on my bed with my new treasures stacked around me, I'd opened it curiously, wondering at the accident that had left it in a box where it did not belong, and puzzling at the homemade cover and odd typeface. Had read the inscription;

For you who are, who have been, and who will be — we are one.

Flying miles above, and even further beyond, anything I'd recognize as home, thirty years after puzzling over that inscription of "we are one" for the first time, I'd read those words again and felt my throat tighten with remembered emotion and present sense of loss.

The dying light behind us had glanced off a wing just then and slanted up to blind me, tears coming, not from light-blindness, but heart-blindness. There was some truth my heart once knew, but the knowing is gone. It was written in this book of "truths" that rested in my limp hands, but it wasn't there for me anymore.

Sitting silent while Tom navigates the open highway between the airport and home, I realize I don't remember the rest of the flight. As the flight attendant had announced our final approach, I'd wiped tears I didn't know I'd cried away from my cheeks. The book lay open on my lap, fingers, cold and stiff from immobility, resting on a page I didn't remember turning to.

If your eyes are full of tears from your past, your future is likely to look blurry.

Really? I'd thought, in a head voice rich with sarcasm. You don't say?

I keep seeing those words as I shower and climb into bed, tears of pain and exhaustion still threatening my vision. My blond fluff of a cat is already there, kneading my pillow to suit her liking and purring like a jet revving for takeoff. No mistake about it, I've been missed. The little tom cat is more distant, he's curled at the foot of the bed pretending not to notice that I'm home, giving his ecstatic sister a skeptical side glance as if to say, "*You* can get excited if you want to, but I'm going to make her beg *me* for attention, not the other way around."

I pet them both, delighted by their individuality. Suki can't *not* purr; I can feel the vibration in my toes where he's lying at the foot of the bed, although

I can tell he's trying to squelch it. Taffy revs her motor up a few more rpms and snuggles into the curve of my neck as soon as my head is on the pillow. We sleep.

The dreamer recognizes herself now, in slide shows and fuzzy home movies shown on the screen of my closed eyes. Racing down dirt roads and alleyways on horseback, mane, tail, and braids flying in the wind created by our motion. Glimpses of myself as a toddler, happily trampling game boards and puzzle pieces laid out on the floor by my older siblings. And always the slim figure of the girl, with her peaceful warrior's face, her graceful waiting stance, and her watchful eyes.

She isn't part of my memory, only my dreamscape. My dreaming self accepts that this is right. All is as it should be.

This life of car to plane to desk, followed by plane to car to home takes a toll. Add in sleeping in hotel beds with hotel pillows, short nights followed by early mornings, and it isn't surprising that Saturday often finds me tired, achy and thoroughly out of sorts. The only cure I know is fresh air, yoga, and a brisk walk.

I don't *like* living in the suburbs. No open fields and uninterrupted sky, no quiet broken by the chirp of a cricket and the shriek of a hawk. No walking to the corner coffee shop or the theater either. None of the advantages of city or country, but this is where I live.

It isn't where I take my yoga classes though. I've found a studio in the older part of downtown, and it's worth the 40 minute drive to spread out my mat and feel the energy of many blessings settle into my bones. Here, I may find some fellow students only interested in the exercise, but most come for the moving meditation, for the open spiritual airways, and for the communion of like souls.

I don't sit cross-legged as easily as I'd like, years of neglecting my health have brought the fibromyalgia that has been part of my life since my early twenties to a level that hampers movement and flexibility. But I breathe into the tight, hot pain that spikes in my shoulders, hips, and knees as I lower myself to my mat, and prepare for meditation and movement.

Savasana. We stretch out on our mats, release the mindful breath we've been practicing, and give everything to the earth. I'm a little chilly, but I don't want one of the rough blankets that the studio keeps on hand. The cooling of my body makes me drowsy, listening to the flute and soft drumming from the sound machine, swimming close to sleep. I often see colors when I'm in yoga practice, oranges and purples, aqua and emeralds, unfurling in my closed-eye blindness like swaths of rich silks backlit with sunlight and flowing like water. Today, all I see is the flame red cotton of the sundress the child wore on the prairie and again in my dreams. How long, I wonder, will that chance vision haunt me?

Being honest with myself, I have to admit I don't feel haunted by it. Mystified, yes. But I'm beginning to associate her presence with a calm sense of safety. Rolling up my mat and sliding it into its nylon bag, I think how much *I* would have loved wearing that dress when I was thirteen. I love the rich color and the sweetheart neckline and especially the flared skirt that seems almost magical in the way it responds to her every movement. Whoever my little warrior is, I laugh to myself, she has fabulous fashion sense.

Somewhat restored, muscles letting go of their stubborn knots, I feel like a walk in the park would be just the thing to bring me fully back to human status. There is a haze of early spring mist in the air, but a little moisture won't do anything but make my hair curl, and today I don't care how I look.

The nearby park, almost exactly a quarter mile on each side, is bordered by a sidewalk and a wrought iron fence that might have begun its life two centuries ago in New Orleans. Its heart is full of winding paths, old trees, flower gardens, fountains, statues, and benches.

It draws me like an ancient hymn, still hummed, but neglected so long I've forgotten the words. I throw my mat in the trunk of my car, pocket my keys, and walk the two blocks over to the park. Not many people on the sidewalk that runs the outside edge of the park today. The usual weekend walkers, joggers, and moseyers must be waiting for the drizzle to stop.

Any experience can serve to bring you more deeply into yourself. But a powerful yoga practice, shared by a few people who are also reaching deeply into their own essence, is a magical place to begin. I feel myself slipping back into the spirit space I usually only experience on the mat. If I can just hold onto the magic a little bit longer.

I pull up the hood of my jacket against the wet and, matching my stride to the hum of the hymn in my head, I set off, toes landing on the sidewalk at the northeast corner gate. I move south, muscles still warm from my time on the mat, the tingle of power from my core reaching into my legs as they bear me forward, into my arms as they swing a counter rhythm to my steps.

Second day of spring and barely 40 degrees. The sunny skies and 60 degree weather I'd left in Kansas might find its way to us next week. The park is preparing for it, tight green droplets and red knobs are showing on the oaks and redbuds.

The drizzle is increasing to a steady drip – I reach for the magic of words, hoping to capture some of this magic before it dies away and before the weather puts an end to my moving meditation.

Water, the element of our birth, collects on my face. Wind, element of momentum, has pushed my hood back and is now toying with my damp curls. Earth, element of our foundation, aches with the rebirth of the season to push up the seeds and bulbs that have tarried there during the winter, straining even at the sidewalk under my feet. And where is Fire? Where is that element of our yearning and desire, embodiment of our lifeforce?

In answer, Fire awakens in my belly, blossoms in my heartsong, blows through my mind, and burns through veins and neurons, rivulets of light streaming into the soulscape that the park is for me today. Today, *I am the fire!*

Past the gates at the southeast corner. Turning west, moving fluidly as I am seldom able to do these days, since moving most often heralds pain. Rhythm sets my breath alight, pulls me forward, wanting only to feel my foot touching the earth, the air filling my lungs, the water soaking my hair, and that fire at my core warming me even on this wet, cold, unspringlike day.

I feel my feet striking the ground as I would a stick striking the drum, an accent on a melody that begins where I begin. A nod to the gates at the southwest corner, turning north. On the last quadrant, turning east, I'm marking the four corners in a ritual as old as the world and as new as the instant I move through.

The wind is stronger, in my face now, and I'm thoroughly soaked, but the magic of the rhythm and the elements is still surging through me. I turn away from the crosswalk that would take me to my car and begin the journey south again.

Lost in the magic of my elemental reverie, I almost don't notice when he falls into step beside me. He's young and lithe, a dancer's bounce in his step as he matches me stride for stride. I throw him a startled look. He smiles at me, flashing gold in his front teeth and a sparkle in his eye before he faces forward again. His hair is dripping wet too, and I'm sure it would out-curl mine if it weren't twisted into dreadlocks. He's lightly dressed for this weather, long sleeved tee and loose nylon running shorts. I think I've seen him before with some of the guys who work out in the nearby community center.

"So I gotta ask," he opens the conversation, "are you a trainer?"

Startled from spirit-space to here-now conversation, I'm baffled. "Huh?" is the most articulate response my mind will frame.

"A trainer," he repeats. "You're out here moving right along in this rain, you're totally in the zone, you look great, and I'm pretty sure I know you from somewhere, so I figure you must be one of the trainers."

I realize he is referring to the athletic trainers at the center. As if! Most days I can't move across the room with grace, let alone set this brisk, rhythmic pace around what equates to a one mile track. I shake my head and gaze mutely back at him.

He's looking me over a little more closely. In my yoga pants and running shoes, hair pulled into a pony tail except where escaped strands curl defiantly around my face, hooded jacket with the logo showing prominently over the left breast, I might be dressed for the part. Surely he can see on closer inspection that I don't look like a trainer. But he only says, sounding surprised, "No, I don't know you, do I?"

I expect him to apologize for mistaking me for someone he knew, or wanted to know. I expect him to pick up his casual pace and start jogging in earnest, ending our conversation as quickly as it had begun.

Instead he says, "I like your energy. Mind if I walk with you?"

"Not at all," I assure him. "You'll keep me from getting lazy."

"So do you train at the center?" he asks. Apparently he is determined to mistake me for a serious athlete. "I box," he continues, seemingly without the need for a breath in between. "Been boxing since I was a kid, got an eleven-year-old brother who's boxing now. He's pretty good."

"I'm 26," he adds. "You're what, 30? Maybe 31?"

I have to laugh at this attempt at flattery. It's been a while since I've been hit on by a stranger. Maybe my instincts are still on that otherwhere plane with the elements, they sure hadn't warned me about this one.

"Thanks, but no." I tell him, adding a silent "no thanks" at the end. It's not that he's black and I'm not, or that he's actually nineteen years my junior. I'm just not in the market or on the market.

"I'll be 45 this summer," I add. Not that it's any of his business. But it might dampen whatever fire he's got burning. At any rate, it's the truth.

"No way!" His surprise seems genuine and he's laughing, like I'd pulled a fast one on him. Or tried to. "Not possible! You *might* be 35, I'll give you 35, no more. I've got an aunt that's forty, no way are you older than my aunt."

"You'll have to give me all 45, I've earned 'em." I keep walking, I don't care to have a conversation about my age, but I'm not going to suggest another subject either.

"Well, you're looking great for 35," as though I had not just restated my age. "Your *energy* doesn't feel that old. More like my age really. You've got a light thing going on, it *feels* young!"

A "light thing?" Oh boy, first flattery, now he's going to go for complimenting my aura? I walk a little faster, not thinking I can out pace-him, but maybe he'll have to save his breath for walking instead of talking nonsense.

Not even close. He easily matches my stride, his voice still strong and sure, not the least bit winded. "I train four times a week, usually in the afternoon. Maybe we can walk together more often."

What, like we've been walking together now and then, and he wants to make it more frequent? His causal air suggests that I will have no objection. He isn't asking, he isn't telling, he's just offering what he assumes will be a welcome suggestion. I find that it is. He has a pretty strong vibe himself, and it's cheerful and sunny in spite of the rain that still drips down my neck. Good company as long as he drops the silly compliments.

"I go to school too, working on my bachelor's. *Finally!* And I do some construction for my uncle. I move stuff for people, TVs and furniture and stuff. And I've got the fight money, I'll be fighting in the Golden Glove match, wanna come? I'd love to have you out there, give me a reason to make it look good, do my best, you know?"

I try to catch my breath enough to answer, this pace has me winded, and he's not even breathing hard.

Before I can say a word, he's off on another tangent. "I want to get a degree, it's the right thing to do. And I'm saving my money for when something big comes along – a business, real estate, whatever it might be. Fighting's okay, it's fun and the training is good discipline, and you can win stuff, even money. The stuff is cool, but it's the money that's going to put me on my path. What I really think I'll do is preach, you know, like be a minister or something."

Now that *does* take my breath away, and makes every muscle in my body tense. I have nothing against any faith, I consider myself a deeply spiritual person, but I have mixed emotions about my experiences with preachers and organized religion. This young man bounding next to me with his easy stride and cheerful voice, his dreadlocks and earrings, doesn't fit any of my notions of preacherhood.

"I feel like God gives me so much," he goes on, appearing not to notice the tension suddenly between us. "I mean, I'm healthy, I'm smart, I got friends and people who care about me. Lots of good people out there. I like meeting people. I figure God is good, he ain't gonna introduce me to any bad people." Here he gives me a sidelong grin as though his theory has just validated my inherent goodness.

"But lots of good people get kinda confused about their goodness, you know? Like they need a little reminder, from someone they can hear. You know *I* don't care if people are black or white, rich or poor. I *liked* livin' down here in the city. I was born around here, but we moved out to the 'burbs. I still come here to train because I like to meet all the different people. And down here people don't really care if you're Mexican or African or Asian or Indian. 'S all the same, pretty much. But all over, I meet people who won't listen to anyone who's not like them. And so I figure there's some that will hear *me* that might not hear anyone else.

"I feel like I want to pass on what I got," he adds. "I want people to feel what I feel when I wake up in the morning and think, 'Wow, I'm so happy to breathe!'"

Happy to breathe! What a simple statement, except it isn't. It isn't just that he's euphoric at having another day with air in his lungs, it's that he's so certain of his purpose, to share that perspective and the joy it gives him with others.

I'm listening closely now, fears of being hit on or preached at all forgotten.

His sincerity seeps into the air around us. I'm going to have to slow the pace soon or I'll collapse right here on the sidewalk, but the more he talks and the more animated he becomes, the quicker his steps.

Just as I think I'm going to have to beg for mercy, he stops and holds out a hand. "I'm Vincent," he says.

I offer my hand, long chocolate-shaded fingers completely cover it. "I'm Dixie.

"Know why God only introduces you to good people?" I ask him, not knowing if I know the answer until, suddenly I do. His head is shaking but his eyes are twinkling.

"Because that's what you ask for, to be introduced to their good."

Having given Vincent a truth I hadn't had before, we finish lapping the park in a companionable silence and at a more reasonable pace.

APRIL

"We've got to stop meeting like this," I tell Vincent as he falls in step beside me just as I pass the door to the community center one Monday afternoon. "It might become an addiction."

He laughs, a full-throated laugh of delight. The spring sun is slanting through branches fully loaded with buds and baby leaves. What a difference a couple of weeks have made.

"I've known worse things to be addicted to," he counters. "Never gotten hooked, but I've sure seen it. What are you really afraid of? That I might talk you into training with me?"

"I don't think I could." I'm serious now. "I can't imagine learning to hit people. Kind of violates the golden rule you know, since I don't like to *be* hit."

He throws me an unreadable look and I wonder if he heard something in my voice. But he doesn't comment. "People might talk," I go on. "Your peeps might give you shit for hanging with a middle-aged white girl."

Now the glance is amused, and he adds a wink. "They're all jealous," he jokes. "Every one of 'em wantin' to know how I got so lucky. I tell 'em it's nothing to do with luck – everything to do with brains. If I'm the one smart enough to latch onto the sunshine when it's pouring down rain, then I'm the one gets to do the basking."

I know he's referring to the day we met, that rainy day when the only sunshine was the fire in my core that had been ignited during yoga class and had carried me a total of four laps around the park before I had to call it quits. He'd quit when I did, although I knew he wouldn't consider that walk a real workout.

We'd gone over to the little coffee shop on the far side of the park and hugged steaming lattes and talked for another hour. A late lunch crowd had come and gone, and we had barely noticed. Our lattes had gone cold, and we'd absently sipped the last of the foam without noticing that either.

I can't remember what we had talked about, exactly. But when he asked if I walked there often, I didn't mention the 40 minute drive from my house to the park, or even the yoga studio that brought me to that part of the city. I only said, "When I can. How often are you here?"

He'd told me the days he trained, during the week he finished his training around six o'clock, and I'd told him that if I was in town I'd try to catch him to share his cool down walk. We'd waved goodbye like friends of long standing and took it for granted we'd see each other soon.

So we walked, and we talked.

He did most of the talking actually. More of a philosopher than a preacher, I decided. He saw the world as a sunny, rosy place full of hope and possibilities. He'd seen plenty of things that would give him reason to doubt it, but so far he still held to the idea that all things were possible if you only believe.

Today, he's still on a natural high from his practice rounds in the ring, while I'm holding the fire built during yoga practice. I let him ramble, working off his adrenaline, saving my breath for sustaining the flow of energy from my fiery core to my limbs, and for keeping up with his long stride.

I listen to his bright dreams: boxing matches to win, education to soak up, people to help. I'd love to believe in his world of hope and possibilities, but my mind returns to the men building the Kansas castle, stone by stone. I don't think *that* was what they dreamed of when they were told the war was over and they could go home. I hope Vincent never knows that feeling of dreams that die aborning.

I may still be grieving dreams that died aborning, but my nighttime dreams, when they come, have been full of joy and laughter. Part dream, part memory, I'm enjoying my childhood romps through days of sun and nights of freedom. It's like I'm being shown a path back to me, reintegrating discarded bits of self that defined me, then slipped out of conscious thought.

Like the dream of Midsummer Night's Eve. I see us as soon as my eyes are closed. Ten-year-old me, slipping soundless out the front screen door. Holding the knob and my breath as it snicks closed, a sound barely noticeable against the backdrop of crickets. Her, rising from her cross-legged seat on the porch where she'd been hidden in the shadow of the rioting clematis vine that protects the western-facing windows during the day.

No need for protection from the sun now. It set at least two hours ago, and the only light is the faint ambient glow from neighboring houses, the stars, and a slender crescent moon.

She slips close and takes my hand, the way sisters do in movies, but something I've never experienced in real life. We stay close to the trellis where the green vines hide us from any eyes that might be looking out the windows. Those vines will be covered with tiny, sweet-smelling stars in the fall, but it's just now high summer and they are devoid of flower or scent.

Once past the house, we break for the road, cutting at an angle to stay out of the sightline of the north-facing picture window. We've done this before. The adult me vividly remembers nights of restful wandering or explosive runs taken in dark hours when adults expect little girls to be safe in their beds asleep.

In the dream, I watch our steps slow. We hug the edge of the road, ready to dive for the ditch should the lights of a car show in the distance. As we walk, we pass house after house, most of them showing little or no light, all of them remembered by my dreaming self.

From several of the houses, shadows appear. Dogs, left free to watch over property and human owners, coming out to see if we warrant sounding an alarm. None bark, they all know our shape and smell. Several choose to join us on our ramble, the dreamer laughs to watch what I had never realized then — a housebreaker could have had a heyday the nights I went wandering. Tucked into their beds, safe in the false belief that their faithful companions guarded their sleep, our neighbors would have been amazed to see dog after dog running to greet us, happily abandoning their posts to join our little band.

Like a pair of pied pipers, we reach the end of the asphalt, continuing on the lightly graveled country road with dogs ranging behind and to the sides of us. As we pass Bob Common's sprawling ranch house with its attendant barns and sheds two shaggy shapes come trotting out, tongues lolling. I hear a nicker from the pasture, the gold and blond dappled pony wants to come along.

The dreamer fills in details from memory. The pony's name was Prince. He was a small-boned Shetland of dappled gold with a mane and tail of silver, long and wavy enough to fulfill any little girl's fantasies of fairy ponies. Deep in my dream, I wonder if he knew it was a special night and was begging to come dance in the circle with us as any fairy pony would want to do.

And we do dance. Following my dream on happy waves, I know we will.

More details fill in. Reading my first Shakespeare play, written for a child prince, but seldom introduced to children anymore, I'd discovered Oberon and Tatiana, and the precocious Puck. I'd pronounced them instant friends and, having discovered the date that Midsummer Night's Eve was traditionally celebrated, I vowed to go in search of them at midnight.

So I see our little band searching. The oddest search party there ever was.

The girls stroll awhile, heads close together, arms wrapped around each other's waists. The dreamer sees the pair, but the conversation isn't clear in the dream. Instead, I hear a distant fiddle. And the trill of pipes.

"Listen," I say to the girls and the dogs. But they mosey on, the dogs following scents and hints of strangers and critters, the girls sharing sister secrets that I do not remember ever knowing.

They must be following that sound after all. They turn off into a pasture, the music becoming a little clearer as they walk.

Then, there it is. Lying just outside the shadow of the hedge row, full in moonlight and starlight. A circle.

The grasses are laid low, while tiny purple and white stars flower, unflattened.

The girls step lightly into this fairy ring, and joining hands, they begin to weave, marking out the circle with bare feet, faces tilted back to laugh with the moon.

I'd woken gently from that dream. Finding the little red book and journal still in my hands, I'd closed them with tender care and a sense of capturing the dream, a pressed flower within their pages.

Laying my head back on the pillow, I'd slept a deep, enchanted sleep that took me through to a pain-free morning. I'd hummed the fiddle tune under my breath all day, and gone to sleep that night full of hopeful anticipation of another happy dream.

So the week passes, days of work and walking. Nights of playful remembering. By Friday evening, I'm tired, but happy.

I stop at the grocery on the way home, pick up some plump chicken breasts, onions, and brie. I'll caramelize the onions and stuff them into the breasts with the cheese. Finished with a brandy-laced reduction and served with a lush Pinot Noir it will be divine. It's one of Tom's favorite dishes, making it a perfect end to a perfect week.

I find I'm still humming the fairy fiddle tune as I set the table.

Dream time continues to move me forward and back through my childhood. I now recognize myself in the precocious toddler, the contemplative child, the golden light-filled spirit that my memory says I was. And always, my red-dressed warrior is there with me.

I'm still not sure what she represents, what she is. My guide? My protector? My better self? She's all the things I'd wanted to be. Slender and graceful. Composed – even serene.

I've finally settled on thinking of her as a friend I'd never met, a sister I'd forgotten, a twin soul whose physical appearance belies an ageless ancient wisdom. I love to test my theories of the universe against her implacable countenance, lying with my eyes closed, seeing her nod gravely as I formulate personal truths and all-encompassing rules of existence in the non-space behind my eyes.

It's because of her that I open my little red book more often now. Usually I read a page or two, close my eyes and start a conversation. She is always with me, never missing a beat, reflecting back truth as I dive into my ideas.

"Maybe this is why this never feels like home," I say to her, having turned to my little book and found the words:

The spirit lives in a deeper place than our beliefs. But our _beliefs_ can block the way to our connection with the spirit.

I'm clumsy with it. I've never tried to put it into words, the *knowing* that my experience in the here-now is only the surface of a pool encompassing infinity. "I don't mean this house, or this country, or even this planet. I mean this whole getting born and living and dying in this plane of existence. I don't believe that's true. I don't really exist here. I'm not really female, or male. My body doesn't really hurt. I don't really need this bed to hold me up, and this bed isn't really here either. I am not really a consultant and what I teach people doesn't really make them money because money isn't real. This can never feel like home because it isn't real. I don't even feel like I'm real here. Is that a belief that's blocking my connection with the spirit?"

I tell her about the nights before she came to visit my dreams. Nights when I lay unsleeping, staring at the dots on the backs of my eyelids, or at the little reflective cutouts of moons and stars on the ceiling above the bed. Feeling the hot, sharp pulsing pain in my shoulders, elbows, hips and knees, letting myself fall into the nothingness that is everything, knowing that, in that place, I am whole and perfect.

"*That* is home," I tell her. "I know that's *true*, but I can't say why. That pool is like an underwater kingdom, so deep in the sea that mortal humans have never even suspected it's there. And when I'm still and open, I can dive there. Like a mermaid going home."

She's wearing a wistful smile now, head inclined slightly and nodding. She's been to those depths I'm sure. I suspect that's where she is when she isn't answering my call for comfort and companionship.

"Maybe that's true of mermaids too. Maybe they really *do* live in some infinite sea below the ocean that we think of as *real*. Maybe it's even true of all the things we think are myths – Pegasus, and unicorns, and fairies, and fauns.

"Or are all stories true?" I demand of her. "Are they all memories? Or at least possibilities? If this isn't home, and this life isn't real, then are those stories as real as my life? And if this place isn't home, if none of us are real here, is dying the only way to go home and be real again?"

She doesn't answer. I'm not asking her to. I'm thinking about the story of the little mermaid who sacrificed everything she was for love. I wonder if she was a denizen of that deep-lit-everything-in-nothing place I visit in my dreaming wakefulness. Did she come to remind us of the magic, to play in the not-real waves, to sing us home only to forget and to fall in love with the illusion?

I'm blanketed in peaceful sadness for that little lost mermaid. Knowing that her loss is only part of the *story*, not part of the reality. Knowing too, that in letting myself feel for her, and with her, I access the magic in my soul and open the pathways to that place I once knew as home. That the truth of her story is in the mark it leaves on each person who hears it.

I'm deep enough in reverie, far enough away from the now-time I share with this illusion of a girl, that I almost miss her response. "Does it matter? If the stories are true?"

"Maybe not," I murmur, "but most people would think I'm crazy for believing it."

Her soft husky voice is the last thing I remember before I slip into sleep. "Sanity is too high a price to pay for growing up."

I am not surprised, the next morning, to open my little red book and read;

Sanity is too high a price to pay for growing up. They may call you crazy – never believe it. They may call you sane – never value it.

I grab my journal from the bedside table and pull the cap off of a felt tip pen; purple today, the red one ran dry yesterday.

In it, I scribble my translation;

Always be willing to make up stories. Always keep growing. Always challenge everyone's truth – including your own.

Something like that anyway, I think, reluctantly pushing back the covers. Time to get this day started. The yoga and frequent walks are helping my pain levels, but mornings are still my least favorite time of day. Not that I was ever a morning person. My mother always said I was impossible to get to sleep, but at least I never woke anyone up early.

Which hadn't kept me from waking them in the middle of the night. They said I had an "overactive imagination" – what they meant was I had nightmares that would have made a horror-movie script writer rich beyond his wildest dreams. My outbreaks of "imagination" also made my parents desperate to keep me from waking the entire county with my screams.

Some dreams were one night shows, some had recurring runs in the theater of my mind until long after I was grown and married to Tom. Even then, some of the dreams that visited me again and again weren't dreams at all, but memories. Like the one I'd dreamed last night.

I knew as soon as I saw the tree. An old sprawling oak, limbs perfect for swings, and a trunk that three small children holding hands could not encircle. I know, because we tried, Mike, Mina, and me.

It stood in the backyard belonging to our neighbor to the east. It reached across our pasture fence, and in later years shaded my horses as they stood, limp-hipped, swishing at flies with lazy tails.

In this dream, the tree is home to a crude tree house, little more than a platform perched precariously in the crotch of two main branches. Slats nailed into the trunk provide a ladder of sorts. At the base of the tree is a dark-haired boy, dancing from one foot to the other, and me, age five, standing with one hand on the bottom slat, looking up. On the platform, several feet above us, an imp of a girl sits, short legs dangling over the edge.

The dreamer remembers them. Mike and Mina, the neighbor's grandchildren, visiting for the summer. Mike, a year or two older than I, excitable and easily inspired to mischief. Mina, a year younger, slyly persuasive and the source of much of that mischief. Their grandmother doted on them and would do almost anything to bribe them to stay the entire summer. I know I'm distracting myself from what is coming next by wondering what has become of them.

No matter, the movie has begun, the plot unfolds. Mina beckons tauntingly, "If I can do it you can too." Beside the girl that I was, Mike urges, "Go, go, I wanna go after you!"

She climbs.

Our little burg looks different from this vantage point. I hadn't yet learned to climb the pear tree at home, so I had never seen our streets from this height before. She stands on the platform, absently twirling the end of one braid around her finger. I'd get in trouble for that habit too, I remember. A third grade teacher threatening to cut off my braids if I didn't stop playing with them. I'd been nearly hysterical at that, a response she had never understood. But there I go, trying to pause the movie again.

"Dixie, time to come hoooooome." Tuned to it as she is, she hears the voice before they do. He always booms it that way, the word "home" taking at least three syllables of space in the air.

The dreaming me almost laughs at the way the little-girl me stomps her foot. No question of whether or not she will obey, but she isn't going meekly.

"You can't go, you just got here." That's Mina, used to getting her way in all things, no concept of being made to do something she really doesn't want to do. "Just tell him you didn't hear him."

Mike is hanging from the trunk, hand firmly gripping the slat a foot or two from the platform.

"I have to go." Thick with disgust, her voice isn't any more meek than the stomping foot. Another warning bellow makes both the dreaming me and the child me jump, "Dixie, come hooooome NOW!"

She's moving to the edge of the platform, expecting the boy below to give way. Instead he laughs up at her, tightening his grip on the slat.

"Mike, move! I have to go home, or I'll get in trouble." Her voice is edged with panic. I'm tense in my bed, fighting to wake.

"Make me," he challenges. Even dreaming, I know he means no harm. "Getting in trouble" to Mike and Mina meant being sent to your room, or if you'd been *really* bad, perhaps grounded for a whole day. The dreaming me knows that even the little girl I'd been is not expecting what is to come, these two can't imagine an adult being mad at them for more time than it takes to work up a tear or two.

"Just move, you're going to get me in trouble. Please?" She's pleading now.

"Mikey move," finally Mina takes her side. "Moveitnow!"

Accustomed to taking direction from his strong-willed little sister, Mike moves. She's down the makeshift ladder in a scramble, knees and hands scraping against the ragged bark and gathering splinters from the rough slats. As soon as her feet hit the ground, she's racing across the yard, over the path beside the ditch, in through the back door.

He is there already. She's begging as she skids to a stop. "Iwasupinthetree. Mikeywouldn'tletmedown. I'm sorry. I'm sorry."

The child doesn't register it at first, but the dreamer knows it's there. A skinny limb from my beloved pear tree, hanging from his right hand. He grips her arm with his left and drags her through the house. I don't remember him saying a word then, maybe he didn't; he is silent now. Not until he throws her, still protesting her innocence, onto my childhood bed, does he speak.

With the first lash of the pear switch he bursts out, "I *told* you to come home!"

Swish. The leg where it connects explodes with hot tingling pain. "I told you NOW!" Swish!

She makes it to her feet, the mattress giving at each desperate step, the lashing whip reaching her wherever it can. His voice again and again, "I

TOLD YOU!"

Teeth clenched, jaw set, dancing away, jerked back by a hand that catches the tail of her skirt. Thrown to the bed, stiff with anger, feeling the bubble of skin where welts form in hot lines across tender flesh.

She's through protesting, through explaining, through begging. No more tears, no more reasoning. Just anger - bright, cold, clean. She's consumed by the sense of betrayal, the injustice. He wants her to admit she was bad; he wants her to be sorry. Well, she's *not* sorry. She's not sorry because she didn't do anything wrong.

I don't remember him stopping.

Even in my dream it seems to be an eternity before he stops and throws down the pear limb. Back in my dreaming mind, seeing with adult eyes, I realize that the red I am seeing is partly the flame of the dress on the figure standing beside my bed. She isn't looking at me. Her eyes are focused on my father's face and her head shakes slowly, sadly, from side to side.

The little girl I was has collapsed onto the bed. Her eyes are fixed on him too, but her face flames with defiance. No sadness, no fear, only recognition of the gauntlet thrown and complete engagement in the battle. If I didn't know what that engagement was going to cost her, I'd have had to laugh to see that little bit of a girl glaring her challenge at the powerful man who stands over her.

It's the expression on *his* face that takes my dreaming self aback. His gaze is fixed on a spot over my head, meeting the eyes of my warrior sister. His face is a study in tragedy, lips set in a thin line, nostrils pinched, eyes pleading. Without a glance at the figure crumpled on the bed, he turns on his heel and walks away.

Poor Tom, I think as I turn on the taps in the tub, a shower isn't going to uncoil my muscles enough to get me through this day. He'd put up with the dreams and the night shakes. He'd learned not to panic when he woke in the night and found me gone, off to wander the streets in search of nothing I'd ever found. He'd gotten careful about pulling off his belt too suddenly, he'd continued to be careful, even when I no longer flinched at the sound. He never complained.

He'd gone with me when I went home to nurse my father through the last stages of bone cancer. He'd never asked me, "Why?"

I can still see him sitting next to the hospital bed we'd brought into my parent's bedroom. Can hear my father's voice listing the equipment, tools, riding tack and harness, even the scraps of metal, wood and leather he'd horded. I listened as he calmly inventoried everything of value he'd accumulated in his life and placed it in Tom's hands, one word after another.

If Tom was baffled that I could offer care and love to the man who more than once left welts and bruises from my shoulders to the backs of my knees, he didn't mention it. He simply followed my lead and gave his love and attention as freely to my family as had he given it to me.

And when, before checking into the hospital for more useless tests, my father had said to him, "If I get to come home from the hospital, I sure would like to see you kids married," Tom simply said to me, "We're getting married."

I settle back into the sudsy, scented water, reviewing the dream. Is sanity too high a price? Or is growing up is too high a price to pay for sanity? Living the life of a "sane" adult has certainly taken its toll, on both me and the man I'd married.

The superheated bath is suddenly overwhelming. I need to breathe. I wrap a towel around my wet hair, wincing at the stab of heat in my wrists and shoulders. What about those lines I had written this morning, the aftertaste of the dream still bitter on my tongue?

Always be willing to make up stories. Always keep growing. Always challenge everyone's truth — including your own.

How do I challenge my *own* truth? I stare into the mirror, my face so unlike my father's, except for the pleading in my eyes. If I won that challenge, would I still be sane?

I wrap myself in a light bath robe and escape into the cooler air of the bedroom. She's there before me, sitting cross-legged at the foot of the bed. My little tomcat is curled next to her, paws tucked tight against his chest, tail wrapped neatly around his body. He could be meditating, or dozing. With Suki it's hard to tell.

I look away, look back at the bed. I'm expecting to see the place next to Suki empty. Surely this remnant of my subconscious mind isn't sitting calmly on my bed while Suki, never one to cozy up to strangers, reviews his wealth of universal wisdom and strategizes his next attack on the rodent population.

Well, if Suki can take the physical manifestation of a child warrior in stride, surely I can do the same.

"Will you be sane?" Her husky voice still speaks in my head even though I see her lips moving.

"So am I sane now?" I'm whispering. Now that she's "really" here, I feel like I should speak aloud.

Her mind voice has a hint of amusement. "You don't have to whisper. I can hear your mind, just like before. I thought it might be easier if you could open your eyes to see me."

Right. Why would I think I need to vocalize just because she appears to be in the room with me? Sheesh! This whole "conversing with figments" thing takes some getting used to.

I want to sit. Not next to her. Not where I might find that the body I knew could not be real, actually radiated heat. Or didn't.

I ease myself gingerly to the floor. When I look back up at the bed, Suki is alone. He opens his baby blue eyes, sagely closes them again, and begins to purr.

Definitely *not* sane.

I dress with only a moderate amount of pain. My suitcase is nearly packed. I add my toiletries and move into the office to pack up my computer. This week will be three days gone before I get home again. I'm flying out on a Sunday to give myself a little time to settle in before the whirlwind that is my Texas schedule kicks into gear.

Before my flight home Wednesday night, I will have been in Dallas, Houston, and San Antonio. I will have spoken to hundreds of people, some from a distance in the conference hall and some from far too little distance in the exhibit hall. I will have given dozens of answers, most of them at least close to right. I will have asked dozens of questions, most of them answered with a segment of truth. I will have taken pages of notes, most of them reasonably accurately representing events, if not capturing nuances of meaning.

If I'm diligent and disciplined, I might have written that article that is due the end of the week. If I'm lucky, I might have retained one or more new clients or received new offers to speak, write, or otherwise contribute something for which I will be paid.

All between now and Wednesday night.

I stand, suddenly weary, my little red book in one hand, my computer case on the desk in front of me. I remember my mother's stories of her friend, the little old lady who would sit over her Monday morning tea cup and say, "Today I'll do the baking then tomorrow it's the washing and ironing and then Wednesday I'll do the canning and clean house." And after running down all the chores faced by a country housewife, she'd pause and sigh into her Monday morning tea, "Oh my, the week's half gone, and I haven't done a thing."

I remind myself it is only Sunday, and still nearly four hours before I will, with the help of a hoard of Southwest personnel and one big silver bird, be in the air southward bound.

I'm restless to get started, to get it over with, to come back to the life that has meaning and substance for me. I want to get back on the mat, walk in the park with Vincent bouncing beside me, see if the rose buds are opening or only teasing me. I want to sit over a hot foamy latte and watch the people and their dogs. Watching a dog with their person is as rich to me in story as the park is rich in story to the dogs, with their fine-tuned eyes, ears, and noses.

"Always be willing to make up stories," I repeat to myself. When had I become unwilling to make up stories? When had I learned to care about being "sane?"

Time to make up stories and challenge truths later, now is time for *doing*. I slip my little red book and my journal into my computer case next to my plane ticket and head for the door.

When you are asleep, give yourself fully to rest and dreams so that when you wake you may be fully present. Otherwise, you may find you are no longer truly alive.

So says my little red book on the page that is revealed when I unpack it from my computer case that evening. The other side of the page says:

There may be time to sleep when you're dead. But waiting 'til then to find the time will

Okay, so early to bed for me then. Unpacked, my files for tomorrow's meetings prepared, I order room service.

I don't have a mat with me, but I go through a few sun salutations anyway, arms sweeping up and back, forward and down. I'm surprised to find that even after the flight and stress of getting a rental car, finding the hotel and getting bags up to the room, I can place my palms on the floor after only a few repetitions. The pangs from this morning have faded, and in spite of the emotion of last night's dream, it's been a good day.

Time was, and not that long ago either, a dream like that would have led to days of stiff joints and hot pain, a sick stomach and an aching head. I would have fought the urge to crawl back in bed and, while I've never cancelled a client meeting due to pain, I would have fervently wished I dared to do so.

This morning I had been out of sorts and hurting, but by the time I left for the airport I had almost forgotten the anger and outrage the dream produced. Now I'm relaxed, prepared for tomorrow's meeting, and ready to settle in with a lovely piece of salmon followed by a good night's rest. I sign the slip for my food and move manila folders and my laptop aside to make room for the little red book and my journal.

I'm not surprised to look up and see my spirit sister curled into the club chair. Amazing how quickly I've acclimated to not being sane. I wink at her and, forgetting I don't need to speak aloud, ask, "Want a bite?"

She doesn't give that the dignity of an answer, but she can't help the smile that flickers across her face. I may not know what she *is*, but I know what she isn't. She isn't the sort of being that needs salmon and baked potatoes in order to exist.

"So, what changed?" Her frank gaze flames with curiosity. "Why is this day after a nightmare different from other days after a nightmare?"

My fork pauses midway from my plate to my mouth, its load of luscious salmon forgotten. Slowly I lower it back to the plate.

"I don't know." It hadn't even occurred to me to think about it. "I suppose it's like touching my toes, it's less painful every time I do it?"

I can tell from the question in my voice that there is an important clue here and I'm missing it. I focus my inner vision on the difference, the "now versus then" comparisons. I tick them off on my fingers.

"One, I dream more, but a lot of the dreams are happy memories. I don't know if I *never* dreamed of good times before, but if I had those dreams, I never remembered them.

"Two, I have things to look forward to. I have yoga and walks, Vincent has been a great friend, and, I have you." I glance away, suddenly shy and unsure.

What does it mean that I "have" her anyway? She is always present in my dreams, always there when I close my eyes and look for her, and now we're having a conversation while I have my eyes open and am not in that half dreaming trance where I usually go to visit her. Or perhaps where she comes to visit me.

Without giving her a chance to respond, I plunge on. "Three, I'm healthier. I'm eating better," here I stop ticking off points on my finger and pick up my fork again. Darned if I'm going to let a conversation with a child who doesn't need to eat keep me from enjoying my dinner while it's hot. I take several bites, savoring them fully, before I continue.

"I'm eating a *lot* better," I gesture at my plate, take another bite to stress the point. "I'm exercising more than I used to. I hurt less, I feel more ... I don't know, maybe purposeful. And I'm more creative. I even wrote a poem last week. And I *finished* it!"

That last part was true too. The first thing I'd written just for the joy of creating, in more than a year. I'd danced a little, spinning in elated silliness, hugging my journal to my chest and laughing out loud with the release of having even that one thing full-birthed on the page. No more "died aborning" – it had spilled out of me whole and nearly perfect under the silver glow of the last full moon.

I'd spent the day in a client's office a couple of hours west of St. Louis and had driven home in the early evening. As I got on the interstate, the last rays of the dying sun flared bronze and orange in my rearview mirror. Within half an hour the full moon was rising in front of me, a huge gold disc with dents from a cosmic hammer glinting darker gold. I followed the line it made on the road, nearly running off the highway when it curved away from the moon path laid out by that giant ball of light.

The poem's heartbeat started there, on that busy highway that might well have been camouflage for a fairy road – marked out by the intersection of the last rays of the sun and the furthest running beams of the full moon.

It blossomed, phrase by phrase, as I drove, as I pulled into the garage, as I snagged a snack from the 'fridge to eat while I checked my email. It kept growing as I showered and dressed for sleep, the fabric of it taking on shape and color as I picked up my little red book and my journal and headed for bed.

I never made it to the bedroom. My feet, and the swelling rhythm of the poem, carried me instead to the patio door and out into the moonlight, now cool and silver from a moon high above my head. I stood there in my nightgown, book and journal gripped tightly in one hand, and tilted my head back to stare.

I don't know how long I stood like that, or what the neighbors might have said if they had seen me. But after however long it was, I sat down on the back step and wrote. My pen was possessed, moving in the light that spilled over my shoulder from the living room, and the light that poured onto the page from the sky.

Finished, it was a live thing. It leapt and twirled with me, pressed flat against my chest, the spine of my journal bent back on itself so that I could hold those words to my heart.

The slight figure in the chair is leaning forward, eyes alight. "Read it," she demands. "I want to hear."

I reach for my journal, the spine still creased so that it opens to the place.

I take a sip of water, suddenly nervous. This isn't a performance, but I want *her* to hear it the way my inner ear had heard it when I captured it here on these pages.

I read.

<u>Light Drawn</u>

It's a drawing on kind of thing
Like a gypsy fiddle echoing softly
Off the silver disk of a full moon

Betraying other conversation
It entices my feet to go wandering

From the safe glow of my hearth fire

Loosening other bindings
It tickles my senses until I'm spinning down the
Spangled path the moon paints

Heart singing
Feet flying
Drawn ever on

It's a drawing of kind of thing
Like a familiar profile, glimpsed only as
Bright relief against the stacked blackness of a pending storm

Countering cacophony
It distills my hope into luminous lines
Of sure stillness that silence fearful thunders

Defining my own image
It tugs at my laugh lines until I'm looking upward
Drinking down every drop of sweet rain

Eyes dancing
Ears ringing
Drawn of pure light

It's a drawing out kind of thing
Like a sweetly scented compress, warm with herbs
And wet with steam

Singing like a siren
It coaxes drops of poison rising repentant
To the surface of my seething thoughts

Absorbing what was unbearable
It reflects it back as precious until I'm kneading knots of passion
Watching pearls drop from my hands

Skin glistening
Heart pounding
Drawn finally out

It's a drawing in kind of thing
Like a summer tide that spirals slowly
Toward the inner curl of a perfect shell

Seeking whole acceptance
It laps longingly at each curve
Pulled unfailingly to the core

Discovering safe harbor
It cradles my battered spirit until I'm lying bathed in sunlight
Resting easy on the sea's breast

Mind stilling
Heart lifting
Drawn simply in

Neither of us moves. The only sound in the hotel room is my breath, coming fast. And hers. I hear it as sharp as a seal breaking, the air seems to snap in through her open mouth. I can't remember hearing her breathe. Before now.

Our eyes meet. I know my eyebrows are lifting, even though I haven't intentionally moved a muscle. My mind holds only one word, "Well?"

She nods. A smile comes slowly and with it the release of that long breath. She keeps nodding, the smile spreading, until it reaches her eyes and her whole face is alight.

"Yes."

Just the one word. But it is enough. Locks have broken and dams have burst, and she and I are reduced to sentences of one word and infinite meaning.

Without thought, we're both laughing, feeling that drawing – pulling us on, pulling us in, and pulling free what had been holding us back. I'm not aware of moving, but the laughter has carried us together, we're suddenly sitting on the edge of the bed, arms wrapped around each other and laughing the laugh of the recently pardoned, the laugh of the patient who's been told the test results were a mistake – all is well, and they aren't about to die any time soon.

It's wonderfully odd and oddly wonderful to feel her head on my shoulder, to know that in this waking world I am the adult and she the child. I tighten my arm around her shoulder and rest my cheek on the top of her smooth head. Our laugher eases and fades, but the smile still tugs at my face just the way I had written that it would.

I look down at my lap where her smooth brown-gold hand is holding mine. I have my mother's hands. I paint the nails to make them look not-like, but I inherited her wide palms and short fingers. Suddenly, I am glad to have a mother's hands. I twine my fingers with the child's slender ones and am content.

MAY

The rest of the trip is uneventful.

The weekend is spent catching up on the backlog of work generated by my absence.

I dream no new dreams.

In fact, in the last week I haven't had any dreams that I remember. Client work has kept me busy enough that I have no time for yoga, the park, or my new friend. Messages from Vincent remind me I haven't been for a walk with him in "forever." Stiff hips and shoulders remind me I haven't been on the mat in almost that long.

To make up for last week's absence, this week I've taken to bringing my work to the coffee shop and changing into my running clothes as soon as I can justify closing the laptop. Today I close the laptop before I can really justify it. The light breeze is summer-laden and even working from one of the tables out on the sidewalk isn't enough "out-of-doors" to satisfy me. Spreadsheets can wait, I want to move.

I follow the path to the heart of the park, noticing the changes that seem to happen overnight.

Like the roses. What *is* it about roses?

One day they're just loaded with promise, buds like little teardrops hiding behind jagged leaves. The next day they're dripping jewels of ruby and topaz. Or maybe I just haven't been paying attention. Wasn't it yesterday I wished that they would bloom? Or was that last week?

Today I've tossed my workbag in the trunk and I'm pausing in front of a riot of roses that I thought yesterday-last-week would never bloom. They've lounged in the sun all day and their fragrance is at its peak, teasing at me to come closer, smell, drink it in. I don't even try to resist. I'm down on one knee with my nose in an umber roseheart when a voice startles me to my feet.

"They're magic, aren't they?" It's a voice light with amusement and soaked in honey. The face is a match; tanned, creased, laughing. Indeterminate age, the creases suggest a long life, the smile says he's only just beginning. I've glimpsed him in the gardens, weeding, mulching, pruning, but I've never seen his smile before.

"You're a summer child," he goes on. "You understand roses."

"I think maybe I *am* a rose," I counter, feeling a teasing grin flash across my face. "Maybe I've been a rose in *every* lifetime. A wild rose, a hot house rose, a cabbage rose, or maybe the rose that blooms in *Arabian Nights* – all whirls and swirls and scent. What do *you* think, what kind of rose are you?"

He actually throws his head back to laugh at me. Overcome by mirth, he collapses on a bench placed on the other side of the sidewalk, facing the roses. When he can speak, he says, "Oh I'm a climber, no doubt about it. Gotta get up above everything, see over walls and peek through fences. You'll find me nodding down at you from way up there. But my roots stay grounded. Always."

What fun! I've actually found someone who likes to play my little game of anthropomorphic analogies! Growing up as an only child, living mostly in my own head, I'd loved to watch people and play with words. Projecting people traits onto my other friends, like roses, roads, or rivers, could keep me amused for hours.

"But you're right," I admit, sobering. "I *am* a summer child. I suffer in the winter, but I survive to bloom again."

"Oh no, that isn't the way of the roses!" The animation in his face shifts to agitated concern. "They don't suffer in the winter. They rest. They snuggle down under their blankets of oak leaves and snow, and they dream until it's time to wake. They need that time as much as you need your sleep every night.

"In the fall they breathe deep and slow, then slip into blissful oblivion for a time. In early spring, the dreams come, of the beautiful clothes they will wear when the sun comes again. They get restless with dreaming, wanting to wake and make it true. But they aren't suffering in the winter.

"The truth is, they suffer when they don't get enough to drink or enough sun. Or when no one comes to pull the weeds that steal their food from the soil or to prune away the old blooms and limbs that have become a burden to them. *That's* when they suffer. That's why I tend these sweethearts, to make sure they never suffer and are always dressed in joy."

I'm cemented in place by the conviction in his voice. Like Vincent wanting to help others know his joy in being "happy to breathe," here is a man who knows his purpose. His is the hand and the heart that makes my joy in the roses possible. All I can think to say is "Thank you."

"I do enjoy your roses," I add. "They are certainly dressed in joy today, your efforts are paying off."

"It isn't effort, child. Love is never effort. It's energy, sure. I spend my energy. But it isn't an effort, and the energy comes back to me tenfold. More than tenfold, hundreds, thousands. I can sit and enjoy the roses, but I can also sit and soak up the joy of every person who stops to look and touch and smell. Like I said, they're magic."

I almost expect *him* to bloom. He's sitting back on the bench now, arms stretched along the back of it to both sides, long, denim-clad legs stretched in front, crossed at the ankles. The soft soled moccasins that allowed him to approach without my hearing have a little mulch clinging to them. A climber, alright, even lounging there on the bench, he's stretching to take up every inch of real estate.

I realize I'm staring. I don't have any idea how long I've stood rooted, gazing at this climbing rose of a man and thinking about the joy of knowing, without a doubt, just knowing, what one is here to do.

He pulls in his long limbs and leans forward, returning my gaze. "You're a drooping rose right now," he asserts. "Too long without sun? Or maybe too much rain? You suffered all winter instead of snuggling in to rest? Feeling a little wilty, aren't you child?"

I can't respond. The tenderness in his voice undoes me. I swallow and try to pretend I don't have tears welling in my eyes. He nods, he's seen the heart of the matter, the stunted growth, the overgrown dead brambles, the buds shriveling before they open. The phrase comes again, unbidden, "died aborning." No magic left here.

Birthing that poem had made me think I was healed, the happy blooms restored. Under his shrewd, unjudging eye, I realize that, while there are stirrings of growth, I'm still carrying winter in my heart.

He pats the bench beside him. I sit and let the tears come. He pulls a large, soft handkerchief from his pocket, passes it to me without a word. There, in the sun, watched only by the nodding roses and their gentle keeper, I cry.

Home, in the last lingering rays of the daylight, I venture into my backyard to check on my own roses.

The rose bed is easily viewed from the pseudo-privacy of the patio, which is screened from curious eyes by trellises loaded with that same clematis I'd seen in my dream memory of the ramble on Midsummer Night's Eve. I've carried starts of the same vine with me from place to place. It has always grown and bloomed, and, in every place I've lived, having this vine and a few choice roses always makes me feel like I have at least a *chance* of making a home.

The year before, our neighbors had uprooted their bush roses. I'd come home to see them lying, bare roots on the grass like alien life forms deprived of breath. They were concerned about the blooms attracting bees, they said. They had a toddler just beginning to go out of doors and they didn't want him to be stung.

I guess they thought bees would respect property lines because, when I asked if I might try transplanting a couple of the larger, hardier bushes to my little plot, they were happy to hand them over.

Tom came home that afternoon to find me toiling to extend the existing bed to make room for my new adoptions. He was baffled, a little frustrated, but he took over digging and turning up the sod and suggested that I start breaking up the dirt and picking out the clumps of grass. We worked with a will until the bed was large enough to accommodate two large bushes and a couple of smaller plants.

It was dark by the time we had them tucked in and watered. I'd whispered some encouraging words over my new babies and went in to sleep.

Tom said little about his predictions for my success in resuscitating bare-root roses in mid-summer. But even I had my doubts.

The smaller ones didn't make it. They put out a few spindly efforts, but we finally admitted that they weren't putting their hearts into it.

The larger bushes, however, triumphed. I'd mulched them carefully last October and checked on them anxiously through March and April. The last time I visited they'd been loaded with buds in various stages of preparation for blooming. Today I find that they, no less than the roses under the expert gardener's care, are bursting with joy and blooms.

One is a classic red, red rose – all ruby velvet swirls and a sweet musk scent.

The other is *covered* with miniature suns. I stand now and marvel at the sudden explosions of color.

The stems are long and sturdy, and the blooms are full-circled. I want to wrap my arms around them and smell every sweet, scented heart and kiss every gilded petal. If I needed proof of the restorative powers of winter, these roses are just that substantiation.

I squat there on the grass in front of my little bed of babies, and I think of my newest friend. He'd told me finally, after I'd dried the tears he pretended not to notice and returned his handkerchief without a word, that his name was David.

He'd talked to me in that light bard's voice, rambling on about the ways of roses. "Do you know there are fossils of the rose over thirty million years old?" he'd asked. "And that they've been cultivated for more than five thousand years?

"That one over there," he'd pointed to a sprawling specimen with tiny oval petals. "Probably could be traced all the way back to Egypt in the late second century."

I was soothed by his voice and enchanted by his tales. He wove myth and history together – tracking from stories of the collaboration of Aphrodite and Apollo giving new life to a dying nymph, to the wager between Brahma and Vishnu to decide which was lovelier; the lotus or the rose.

To these, he added stories of the gardens created by Napoleon's wife, Josephine, and the excesses of the Roman nobles who bathed in rose water and strew petals along their walkways while the peasants harvesting the precious rose crop died of starvation.

"Roses and rose water were considered currency once. You could pick a fortune right here in this park if they hadn't fallen out of favor."

I'd had a sense that he was telling me more than story. That we'd picked up a conversation started long ago – around about the time that the rose fossil was in bloom.

"And those things we call thorns," he'd gone on. "They aren't really. Thorns, you know, are actually stems, but the rose just has prickles, like an overgrown epidermis."

I'd giggled, thinking roses really *were* thick-skinned if their epidermis formed such weapon-like overgrowths.

He'd told me of the holy grail of rose growers – the blue rose. And of the ideals and concepts the rose has come to symbolize. True love and pure virginity. Silence, secrecy, and bitter wars. Death, and remembrance, and even the wounds and blood of Christ. Sacred to the Egyptian goddess-mother, Isis, and the chosen emblem of England. It seemed that every culture and every cause had found the rose to be a fitting expression of its meaning.

And here they are, growing happily in the little plot of dirt Tom and I had turned up to receive them. As regal and joyful as their ancestors had been, lifting their whorls of petals in my pitiful little bed as proudly as ever roses had paraded their charms in the formal gardens of royalty and gods.

The air is cooling and the sky deepening to dusk before I leave my rose children and go in to begin dinner. I come out one more time, bringing a pair of shears, and clip a few fully opened blooms for the table.

Sleeping, I watch myself clear the table of dishes. Just as I had cleared the dinner dishes tonight, but this isn't that table, and there is no Tom working with me in easy silence.

I watch idly as then-me washes three plates. We'd eaten off those plates every weeknight of my life for years, saving the turquoise-rimmed china with the creamy dogwood print for the most special company. Washing finished, she picks up a tea towel, the thin, absorbent flour-sack kind, to dry them. Finally, she wipes down the Formica-topped table to make room for an industrial-looking sewing machine.

While there were many evenings that I sewed my clothes at the old kitchen table, I know which evening this is going to be. In these months of dreaming I've learned that the story will unfold the way the story had unfolded, there isn't a thing I can do about it.

As much as I dread seeing the dream I know this will be, some part of me is relieved to have it done. I remember that girl at the kitchen table. I know her face, I know her mind. I remember, too, the skirt that she lifts from a basket and shakes free of its folds.

It's cut from steel gray gabardine, styled to sit close across the hips and flare slightly at the knee. I don't have to look at the skirt in my dream to know that it is finished except for setting on the waistband and stitching up the hem.

I know what is coming when she lays it on the table and crosses to the bureau, reaching for a pincushion shaped like a red tomato. I already hear his voice, and know that when she turns around, the pincushion forgotten, he will be standing in front of her.

"What do you think you're going to do?"

His words cut into the silence like an echo in reverse, I'd heard them in my memory before he spoke them in my dream.

I could wish her quiet, but I don't. What I said then she will say now. I'm not sure me now would make a different choice.

Her defiance is as steely as the gray skirt draped over the edge of the kitchen table.

"I'm going to sew."

Her voice is quiet, controlled, and laced with power. The gauntlet is down. She meets his eyes without a quiver.

"Don't you tell me what you're going to do!"

Now, my dreaming mind says, I'll know what *really* happened. Thirty years later, an event that has stayed with me, playing over and over until I know all our lines by heart, and I still struggle to believe it happened the way that I remember it. If I were truly watching a movie, I'd be sitting on the edge of my seat.

But this is not a movie. Instead of sitting on the edge of my seat, my body is trapped with my dreaming mind, locked unmoving in my bed.

He repeats, "Don't tell me what you're going to do, or I'll knock you right down there on the floor."

She meets his eyes without wavering. "I know you will." Her voice betrays no emotion, only resolve.

They face each other, the man and the nearly grown woman-child. I remember becoming intensely aware of the heat rising from the wood burning stove directly behind me. How we avoided falling into it I will never know.

I watch in my dream as he raises a hand and moves toward her, as she moves backwards, screaming as she almost-not-quite backs into the cast iron stove, moving and dodging his fist until her back is firmly against the wall behind the stove.

She slides along the wall in the barely-enough-space between it and that hot, black monster, nearly to the corner. If she can get around that corner she can slip out from behind the stove, run through the kitchen, and escape out of the front door into the early spring night.

And then he's on her. Exactly the way that I remember. One hand buries itself in her newly washed hair, jerking her head back against the wall. She moves sideways trying to avoid the blow, wrenching herself away from him, sliding along the wall into the corner less than a foot away, collapsing to her knees as he catches her by her hair yet again.

I don't think I'm breathing, but I must still be living, because the dream goes on.

They're both back in the corner now, barely room for the two bodies behind the radiant stove. He's still grasping a hank of her hair in one hand, the other hand braced against her shoulder as he repeatedly slams her head against the wall. The memory is so clear I feel the blows. I see the dots that form on the backs of her eyelids, exploding silently each time her temple connects with the plaster wall.

I can hear my mother's voice, that's one thing that is different. My memory doesn't hold her voice in this scene at all. Even in my dream I can't tell what she's saying. Perhaps just his name over and over.

He is screaming at her now. "Call the cops, she's gone crazy!" He repeats himself, "Call the cops!"

It registers with me the second time. He *believes* I am crazy. He doesn't think what he is doing is wrong. And if he thinks *I* am the crazy one, he might not stop until I am dead.

If I'm dreaming true, I must have gone a little crazy then. I watch her writhe in his hands like a snake. Her eye falls on the poker, lying lengthwise under the stove. She reaches for the barbed tip, stretching until it seems her arm will come out of its socket if she tries any harder. Still the point is just beyond her fingertips.

She fights with words too. The dreaming me is appalled to think that fourteen-year-old me had that vocabulary. Words I don't remember ever knowing at *any* age are pouring out of her mouth, machine gun fire.

The rhythm of her head hitting the wall doesn't break.

I can hear the thud, thud, and see the burst, burst of lights against her eyeballs, although her eyes are now open and fixed on the poker.

I listen for the faint sound of bits of plaster breaking loose, trickling down past the lathe like frightened mice inside the wall. I remember picturing those little bits of the wall, flowing in slow-motion hail inside the microcosm between the kitchen and the living room on the other side.

I watch in horror as the girl I was goes limp, suddenly fearing that the dream will have a different ending than my memory.

Perhaps he fears the same thing, or perhaps he is as worn from the battle as she. He drops her head and gets to his feet, careful of the stove, leaning a hand against the wall above her head to steady himself. She is breathing, I see with relief, her eyes still open, staring blankly at his feet as he moves away from her, past the cast iron monster and the poker lying unmoved beneath it.

The dream freezes there. Just the me that was, crumpled behind the stove, still-damp hair hiding most of her face, hands limp and useless, one in her lap and the other with the fingers almost touching the tip of the poker.

Neither of us cry. Not now.

"He knows," I hear her mutter through the pillow she is holding against her throbbing face. "I think he knows."

"What is it you think he knows, Little One?" The girl I was moves the pillow away from her face to peer at the upright figure of my spirit sister, sitting cross-legged at the foot of the bed.

It's odd to hear "Little One" – they're almost of a size in this time. She maybe a little taller, slim but strong, and the teenage me with the curves gifted me from my German ancestors underlined with muscle gained from doing farm girl tasks. But in this dream that isn't a dream, she still she calls me "Little One" in that soft throaty voice that carries the smile that seldom touches her features.

I watch them from my awake-but-dreaming place, the me-then and the sister of spirit I didn't know I had. Me-now is no one in this little drama, just an interested observer, not even able to cry.

"He knows it's my fault," her voice breaks. "It's my fault that he got sick."

Me-now objects, says, "How ridiculous," remembering that I had told myself even then it wasn't so. I wasn't *that* powerful, to wish someone dead or even ill. I wasn't, I wasn't, I *wasn't*.

But there had been times when I thought I *might* be that powerful. When I felt the energy tingling through my body, and thought it must be how an untutored wizard might feel, coming suddenly into power, with nowhere to send the lightning gathering in his fingertips. I'd look at my hands then, and curl my fingers tightly into fists to keep from pointing them at anyone.

"Explain." The composed face betrays little, but one eyebrow lifts slightly. "How is it your fault?"

"I wished…" her voice is muffled by the pillow she presses to her face again. "I wished he was dead. And I *meant* it!

"Now he has cancer, and he *is* going to die," she lifts her head from the pillow again, but whispers, most of the sound still in her head so that the adults in the next room cannot hear. "He knows he's going to die, and he knows it's my fault. That's why he doesn't love me anymore."

She's ranting, the sobs she hadn't released as her head thudded against the lathe and plaster wall now threaten to strangle her. "I wished he would just die, when he was mad at me and wouldn't stop hitting, and when he made fun of me and when he killed my dog and when…" She can't say the rest aloud, and sobs take over.

I'm begging the then-me to stop. Stop reminding us, stop hating him, stop blaming herself. I want to wake up, but my eyes are already open, staring up at the luminous dots of pretend-stars the previous owners had stuck on the bedroom ceiling, seeing the dots on the backs of her eyelids. And I don't want to leave these two girls alone, one so calm and imperturbable, the other with her face swelling, her hands kneading the pillow, working her way toward hysteria.

I hear my mind-voice saying, "Don't, please don't. It isn't your fault, he's wrong, and you'll learn to forgive him, but it isn't your fault."

She doesn't hear me. Neither of them does. Their two pairs of eyes are locked over the space of the bed, one pair somber but clear, the other darting wildly, showing signs of the blood beginning to pool in bruises around them. They will be black tomorrow. Tonight, she doesn't care about that.

Her muffled sobs and unstaunched tears remind me of my mother's admonition, "If you'd just cry, he would stop." To this day it hurts to cry; crying reeks of being in someone else's power.

"You can change your mind, you know." Her husky voice is that of a reasoning adult. "You don't have to follow this path. You have the power to choose."

I remember our first dream together, her looking down at the pale gold baby and saying, "You're having a reaction, and you can choose."

This time the sea-change eyes that meet hers aren't a calm aqua, they're a blazing emerald, the pupils oversized in the dim light, the whites showing more red than white. This is no innocent baby, trusting her spirit sister to heal her hurts. This is a violently angry child-woman looking to deflect the guilt and horror blossoming in her mind.

The words froth on the tip of her tongue. I hear them as clearly as I know the other girl does, even though the sound she makes is barely a hissing whisper.

"I can *not* choose! You think I'd choose *this*? You think I *wanted* a father who beats me, or a mother who lets him do it? You think I'd *choose* a family without a brother or a sister that's mine even though I have a brother and a sister, and they have each other and I don't have *anyone*. Not anyone! I do *not* belong here. I didn't choose *this*!"

On that last line she lifts her hair from her face to show the ruddy circle above her left temple. My own hand twitches, involuntarily struggling against the dream-trance to touch my own temple where deep creases and a nearly missing eyebrow still mark the aftermath of this night.

"But you did, Dixie." Her delicate face shows concern, but her voice is still reasoning. "You know you did, and you know you're free to make another choice."

Her anger surges out in a mindshout that would have roused the countryside if she had vocalized it. "You're a *liar*. You're like all the *real* people, except you don't really exist. You *lie*, and you make fun of me when I'm hurting. You think I deserve this? Well, so does everyone else, but at least they don't try to tell me I *chose* it! They just tell me if I wouldn't talk back, if I wouldn't run wild like a boy, if I wouldn't read books when I'm supposed to be sleeping, if I'd just *cry*…"

Her voice trails off, then lifts again in even greater fury. "Go away! I can't get rid of *them*, but I can get rid of *you* 'CAUSE YOU'RE NOT REAL! Go away and don't ever, ever talk to me again!"

She throws herself back onto the pillows and rolls over to her side, closing her eyes and burying her damaged face in the bedclothes. So she doesn't see what I see, watching with horrified held breath as the miniature warrior slowly unfolds her legs, slides her feet onto the floor, and stands. Her backward glance is sorrowing but serene as she walks to the window on the north wall, and passes through the glass as though the window frame were, instead, an open door.

I've forgotten the last time the fibromyalgia flared like this. Today is not the nagging ache or the occasional shooting heat. Today, my back is a column of flame, and when I turn the wheel to park the car at an angle to the curb, some invisible demon thrusts a pair of superheated lances into my shoulder blades.

I've missed my usual Saturday yoga class, too slow getting out of bed and into the shower. I'm not even sure why I made the drive to be here. I know a walk might make me feel better, but my knees aren't interested in making the attempt. I'm not even sure my legs will carry me the short distance from my car to the park. Maybe I'll just sit in the sun and try not to think.

I lower myself onto a bench full in the late morning sun. It's like a heating pad against my back and legs, fighting heat with heat. The roses are in full glory, nodding heavy heads on slender canes, wafting perfumes as rich as any high-class courtesan's.

The sun on my face feels good, but the light sets off the old pain in my left temple. That dream should not have shattered me this way. It wasn't like I'd *forgotten* that night. Unlike my other memory-movie-dream nights, this was an event I remembered in detail. An event that had defined my life, severed it between innocence and knowing, between mostly safe and never safe again, between knowing unconditional love and understanding that *nothing* is unconditional.

Each year I worked to put it aside. Finally, I found forgiveness. I tried to reach for peace. Then the effects would show up in my face to remind me. One year the ophthalmologist found a spot on my left retina – "A blood spot, likely from an old trauma?" he'd suggested.

My left eyebrow gradually vanished. "Damage to the subdermal layers," the dermatologist surmised. "The blood supply has been reduced here, the follicles are dying."

A summer of bout after bout of pneumonia, doctors were baffled. I coughed day and night and could barely breathe. Finally, a friend suggested I might consult an ENT specialist. I did.

The phone call with the CAT scan results. "We found a little bit of a surprise. You have a bone spur blocking your airway. How long ago did you break your nose?"

The mystery of my lost vocal range was finally solved. Years of sinus infections from the blockage, toxins dripping down my throat and over my vocal chords. The gaps in my range, the breaks where once I would have nailed the note and held it, I understood the physical damage and the chances that I would ever hit those notes again.

Surgeries repaired the nose, a daily cosmetic regimen replaces the missing eyebrow. I enjoy hearing the songs of others, sitting silent. I no longer even *dream* the harmonies I once created without thought. They have vanished from my head as surely as they have from my throat.

With all of those clues, I had still never connected the stabbing pain in my temple with the old pain of my head connecting with the kitchen wall. Until now.

It was just an event. A thing I survived. An accident of wills.

I'd been dreaming myself into a world where I was safe, where anger and violence were not foreshadowing of things to come but barely remembered anomalies balanced against the bulk of my idyllic country girl life.

Now it is time to face the truth.

I was abused. I was a victim.

Did you really think you could just skip that scene? I scold myself sharply. Did you think you were running the damned projector? That you were choosing the movies? That you could just watch all the happy ones and never see the tragedies?

Needing comfort, wanting someone to blame, I conjure up the warrior girl's serene features.

"Didn't you know that was hiding in there?" I throw it at her, a dare and accusation. "Like that bee," my mind snags on the first of the dreams she and I had shared. "That bee in the rose. You knew didn't you? You *knew* I would be stung!"

The silence in my head hurts more than the anger and fear I've just unleashed. No husky voice answers me, not even with a question. My spirit sister has deserted me. I remember the waking dream that followed. Surely, that too was in the past. She wouldn't abandon me now because I remembered something I'd said to her thirty years before. Would she?

The scene before me mocks my thoughts, I don't belong in this picture postcard. The grass spreads like a lush carpet, neatly trimmed away from the sidewalk. Fountains play in the distance, and a light breeze stirs the upper branches of the trees. And of course, there are the roses. David's faithful nurturing shows in every glossy leaf and satin petal. Heart-openingly perfect, not a single bloom past its prime. Spoiled debutantes, doted on by a loving father, preening in the sunshine.

My pain is an ugly twisted weed, as out of place in the sunbright park as a briar patch among the roses. I stand to leave, my very bones screaming in protest.

I cross the grass, too weary to take the extra steps required to stay on the sidewalk. Being in the shade of the oaks and maples eases the flare behind my left eye.

I can see my car on the other side of the street. It's too far to the crosswalk,

I pull my keys from my pocket and step off of the curb.

I'm almost halfway across the street when I see the flash of yellow. I don't run. I don't pause. The screech of tires on pavement doesn't register until I'm on the ground.

I don't want to move. Don't want to open my eyes. Don't want to be here. I don't want to be anywhere or anywhen. I just want to escape into the dots swimming against my eyelids, pretend they are a universe of stars, dive into them and disappear.

But there are people, and voices. And one of those voices I know. Light tenor, concern rippling through the calm amusement. "What are you trying to prove, child? Invincible you might be, but there's no need to demonstrate it on this plane."

I open my eyes to slits, seeing the moccasins first. I let my gaze travel upward. I squint a little more as dots morph into rays of sunshine haloing his face. David. Rescued by a rose.

I try to stand. I hear protests, but David puts a hand under my elbow, and I manage to get to my feet. To the protestors, I assert that I am fine. To the driver of the car, an anxious middle-aged professor type, strangely stereotypical next to the bright yellow convertible sports car, I apologize. He says he was going too fast, I assure him I was thinking too slow. He says he can't believe I'm not hurt. I assure him it is nothing. David's hand hovers under my elbow, other people drift off to do what they were doing before I offered a distraction.

Finally, the professorish fellow and his sports car pull away.

David stands patiently, waiting for the end of the hubbub. The sun behind him and the pain behind my eyes conspire to blur his features.

"Come, child. Come sit and tell me all about it."

As much as I had felt the need to leave the park, now I feel a desire to return. I'd left it feeling like an intruder. With David's hand hovering below my elbow, breathing in the comforting smell of dirt and freshly mown grass and rose petals and something citrus spicy that is just David or maybe his soap or shaving cream, it feels like going home.

We pause briefly at the sidewalk, David stoops to pick up his basket of tools. He must have been on his way to tend to his babies when he saw my foolish accident.

He guides me to a spot I've never noticed. This isn't where I usually walk. They've placed this bench inside the curve of a flower bed, facing a massive ginkgo tree with a memorial plaque at its feet. Here, the roses share their space with a disheveled baby's breath and late-blooming iris. I sit gingerly, old pain points vying for attention with the new bruises forming from my tumble to the pavement.

He puts the basket down and stands, hands on his hips, looking down at me. I'm grateful for the dappled shade of the ginkgo; I can see him clearly here.

"So how bad is it?" If I weren't listening for it I wouldn't have heard the fear beneath the frustration.

"He barely grazed me," I answer.

"I know that; I saw you go down. But you were hurting already, I saw you crossing the street."

"Oh, it's just the fibro, really. I didn't make yoga this morning, was going to walk here but was just too stiff and sore. No big deal."

For a time, he says nothing. He kneels and begins his ritual, pulling weeds and renegade blades of grass, smoothing the mulch evenly under the treasured flowers. His long arms stretch almost to the opposite edge of the narrow strip of the flower bed. He sits back a little on his heels, gathering up the pile of displaced leaves and roots and tucking them into his basket.

Without looking up he says, "So, this wasn't the first time, was it?"

"The first time what?"

"The first time you tried to die."

He goes on weeding, waiting.

"I didn't. I wasn't trying." Reluctantly, in a whisper, I add, "Not this time."

"Okay." He pauses. "Then why did you slow down?"

I think back on that flash of yellow. If I had moved even one step faster, the sports car would have whizzed by me unfelt except for the displaced air of its passing. One step slower, the front bumper would have taken me square on instead of grazing my leg and throwing me to the ground.

Had I slowed when I saw the car bearing down, going faster than the limit, the driver probably lost in the effect of the sun and wind and joy of pretending to be eighteen all over again? Had I actually wanted him to hit me?

"I didn't know I did." I say, honestly. "I didn't intend to."

David sits back on his heels, wipes the dirt from his hands on the knees of his jeans.

"Do you know your intentions?" His voice is gentle, but there is a steeliness there that tells me he means to be heard. He'll let me evade the question, but the shape of our budding friendship will be warped if I do.

I meet his eyes mutely. He holds my gaze, pinning me against the bench and my fear. Finally, I swallow hard and shake my head. "I don't know, David. So, no, I guess I don't know my intentions. Do *you* think I want to die?"

It's his turn to swallow hard, but he answers bluntly. "The person I see today isn't living."

I'm crying again, I feel tears welling and spilling. It's involuntary, not something I let myself do, not something I can stop. He reaches into a pocket, pulls out a crisply ironed handkerchief by the corner and passes it to me.

It makes me smile, remembering our first encounter. He'd reflected to me in a few words the rose inside, sun starved and twisted back on itself, craving light and room to grow. And I'd sat crying silently on the bench beside him, twisting a handkerchief just like this one in my hands. Had that rose finally died – the truth of my dream the final blow?

Or is it lying, bare root, pruned to only the strongest canes, ugly and twisted, but with all the potential of glossy leaves and fragrant blooms, needing only fertile soil and tender care to burst out like the roses I'd rescued, now in full bloom in my backyard?

I need to tell him. I need to tell *someone*. No, it wasn't the first time. No, I don't want to die. No. I don't know how to live either. But maybe, just maybe, I'm ready to learn.

"David?"

"Hmm?"

"My nickname," I begin where the story begins, with the rose in bud. "When I was a little girl I had a lot of nicknames, but the one they called me most was 'Sunshine.'"

He settles back, I have his full attention. I gather up the threads of story and begin to weave.

"I liked everyone. And I believed that everyone liked me, even grumpy old men who acted like they didn't. And animals. My father said I was going to lose a hand someday because I petted almost every dog I met. But I just *knew* which ones wanted petting. I knew when animals and people were frightened, when they needed to be left alone and when they needed company. I could tease almost anyone into smiling and get almost any cat to purr.

"I didn't feel alone then, I could be with people, or I could watch a bug. After I learned to read, I had my storybook friends. I had cats and dogs, and goats and rabbits and after a while ponies and mules, and there were always the birds to listen to. I didn't have time to be alone. I just wanted everyone to be as happy as I was."

I pause, remembering Vincent's simple statement of purpose, "I just want everyone to feel what I feel, happy to breathe."

David's eyes haven't left my face; he nods for me to go on.

"I *know* it wasn't all 'sunshine and roses.' It's not like bad things didn't happen. My pets died. People died. I cried, but somehow I knew they weren't really gone, just somewhere I couldn't see them anymore. I was still happy.

"I was a handful. I didn't always get my way, and I got in trouble a *lot*, but I was still happy.

"*Really* happy. Sunshine happy."

I take a deep breath and sit up a little straighter on the bench. My hands are clenching the seat on either side, straight arms holding up my aching shoulders.

"Sometimes, when I got in trouble. . ." Here I fight for words. I've told the prequel, now to tell him the real story.

"My father had a temper." I feel myself sneaking up on a thought, a memory, bigger even than the dream. I see the question on David's face, but I don't have an answer. I'm not holding anything back, but I can't share what I can't see.

"I mean ... I know. He abused me."

There, I've said it out loud to a near stranger. A stranger that doesn't *feel* at all strange to me, but a stranger, nonetheless. Maybe it's a breakthrough, but it sounds wrong to my ears.

"I didn't see it that way then. Not until that night."

My voice tightens as I set the scene for him.

"I dreamed about it last night. About the night when everything changed. I was sewing a skirt. I wasn't allowed to wear what was in style, like pants or short skirts, so I had to make a lot of my own clothes.

"I was competing in Speech, my first year, and I wanted a new outfit for the poetry selection I was entered to do. It was actually three poems, all of them about war. So I made a skirt and vest in a blue gray fabric. I thought it would make me look more powerful, more warlike. And I was almost done.

"The competition was the next day and I still needed to set the waistband and put in the hem. My chores were done, dinner was over, and the dishes were washed. I thought surely I was free to do what I chose.

"So, I set up the old sewing machine..." My voice stills. I close my eyes. I see me again, focused on the pincushion, crossing to the dresser to pick it up, the voice behind me, "What do you think you're going to do?"

That question has played in my head, an endless loop, for years. *"What do you think you're going to do?"*

I've been *hearing* it for years. Last night was the first time I'd seen it all. The first time I'd seen how we looked, locked in wits and wills, exploding in physical violence.

I show it to David now, painting it as dispassionately as possible.

I tell him too, what I remember of the days that followed. Wakened early the next morning by my mother, surprised that she expected that I would still go to the tournament, would still compete. Dressing in something that was not my steel blue suit, brushing my hair, just washed the night before, and tying it back into the customary ponytail. I'd be punished, I tell David, for wearing it down. I wasn't going to risk that on this day.

I tell him about the satisfaction I'd felt seeing the swirls of blood where it pooled under the skin around my eyes, blackened like a domino mask above my unblemished lips. Described my left eye, swollen until it barely slitted open.

"I thought no one would be able to ignore that."

My voice stills, my mind wandering ahead.

"I'd like to say I thought someone would rescue me. I *have* said I thought someone would rescue me. But really, I think I wanted to know if what he did was wrong. I knew I was 'asking for it' as he often said. I challenged him, I couldn't be *myself* without challenging him. But I didn't think that being who I was made me bad enough to deserve that."

I sit with that. I listen to the bird song, to squirrels rustling in the leaves. I close my eyes and hear David's even breathing, perhaps I hear the rose petals opening just a little more to the noonday sun.

I open my eyes to see my hands, freshly manicured nails pathetic on hands that show the lines and veins of childhood years of gardening, of chopping wood, of caring for horses and rabbits and chickens. Adult years of scrubbing and cooking, of caring for yards and caring for people. I fold them into fists, the carefully painted white tips disappearing, skin tightening over the knuckles, making them look young again. Almost.

I pick up my remembering. "I trancewalked through the rest of the day. I'd forgotten to bring my folder of poetry, the rules say you have to read it, not memorize it. But I knew it by heart, so I just borrowed some other pages and pretended to read.

"I feel sorry for them now, the other kids and teachers and judges. Except for the kids and teacher from my school, no one knew me. I was just an old-fashioned looking girl in a dress, with long hair and a bruised face. I took my hair down, I tried to hide behind it except when I was performing.

"The first poem was titled *Achtung, Achtung*, and it began 'I am war, remember me.'

"It wasn't asking. It was telling. 'I am war, remember me.'

"I wonder if they do."

"Do you?" He hasn't spoken in so long I'd almost forgotten I wasn't talking to myself.

I open my eyes, surprised that I can. I've been so deep into that past I expect the left eye to stop at a slit, expect both lids to protest at the effort to lift them against the pressure of fluid gathered underneath the skin.

The sun is just passing zenith, the day is hot, although the breeze and the shade of the ginkgo make it bearable. A rivulet of sweat trickles from his hairline and he wipes it away on his sleeve.

I don't answer, we just stare at each other mutely, both of us seeing the story play out in our own fashion.

"I suppose they did their best to forget. I don't remember anyone commenting on my face. Surely, they must have, but I don't remember.

"On Sunday morning, we went to a worship meeting. Most of the people there had known me since I was an infant. And they didn't say a word. They shook my hand, we always shook hands, but they didn't look at me.

"Sunday afternoon there was a gospel meeting. We went. More people who knew me. One woman, she was a nurse and had two girls of her own, reached out and almost touched my face. She looked sad. Then she looked away.

"They were all part of my parents' faith. I suppose you might call it a cult. Or Fundamental Christian. They just call it The Truth. I find that ironic since they didn't much want to see the truth when it was staring them in the face."

David stands and stretches his long frame. Picks up the basket of tools, one corner of it now full of weeds and grasses extracted from where they had snuck into the soft, fertile soil of the bed. He moves to the other side of the bench, sets the basket down and kneels. The rhythm of his pulling and tossing, pulling and tossing, extracting more intruders, freeing the energy and water of the soil to be spent only on the desired plants, is soothing.

Finally, he says, "So, when did you decide to die?'

"When I realized my life didn't mean anything to anyone. There wasn't any reason for me to live." I'm surprised into a true answer.

Monday morning, I'd been sent to the principal's office. Two women from the Social and Rehabilitation Services awaited me. I don't remember the questions they asked, I must have answered them. I only remember the choices they offered when they were satisfied that they had heard enough.

I repeat the list for David now, ticking them off on my fingers. "I was given three choices. I could go into foster care, I could let these women go and talk to my father, or I could handle it on my own.

"I knew I didn't want to be a foster child. One of my friends was an orphan, he was fostered with a local preacher's family. I would never allow what happened to him to happen to me.

"I thought I knew what would happen if they talked to my father. I didn't expect to survive it.

"I'd had time to realize that no one was particularly surprised, certainly no one was shocked. They knew about the previous bruises; these women were only there for me this time because the bruises were on my face for everyone to see.

"No one had cared about the bruises that went before; no one cared now. I'd handled it on my own so far, I'd handle this on my own as well. I told them I'd be fine. I walked away."

I can't stand the hard bench any longer. The cool grass looks like an inviting change. I stand slowly, David starts to rise as well, perhaps thinking I am walking away again.

I wave him down and lower myself awkwardly to the grass next to him. Ah. Down here I can stretch my legs, I can lean backward on my hands and stretch my neck. It feels good.

"No one said anything more," I continue. "Of course, I thought about it a lot. I could only think of two reasonable explanations for the adults to look at me, knowing how I got the black eyes, or at least knowing who gave them to me, and do nothing. How they could *know* it wasn't the first time he'd beaten me, and do nothing. Either they didn't care about me, or they thought I deserved it.

"In the weeks that followed, the bruises faded. The permanent damage was hidden by my young, healthy body. I heal fast. At least on the outside. Inside, the damage spread like spilled ink until everything seemed black.

"I was foolish, I thought it would be easy just to die.

"Did you know that tumbling off the top layer of bales in a polebarn full of hay onto a concrete floor does *not* guarantee a broken neck? It doesn't even guarantee a broken bone! *That* surprised me. And disgusted me, because it hurt. Worse than I hurt now. But two days later I wasn't even limping, let alone dead.

"Same with half a bottle of aspirin. I'd read a book about a girl who overdosed on medicine. But my parents didn't take medicine. Except for the medications my father was taking as part of his cancer treatment and my mother's thyroid medication, there were no pills in the house except the aspirin. Made me sick as a dog, throwing up with the 'flu.' Plus, you can taste those darned things in your nose. Noses are *not* supposed to be able to taste.

"Really, all those stories you read about people killing themselves, it's harder than they make it sound. Not only is it harder, it's darned unpleasant."

I'm trying to bring a little humor back into the conversation. He's having none of it.

"Dixie, it isn't hard at all. Today you almost accomplished it without any effort, without even any *intention*. It's habit forming, this notion of dying. You can practically do it in your sleep."

I flinch away from things I haven't told him. He's right of course. Today isn't the first time I've sleepwalked my way into an accident. The balcony of the hotel on Maui, where I had found myself perched on the outside rail, looking some 20 stories down to the beach with no memory of how I had gotten there. The blare of a bus's horn as I stepped off the curb almost into its path. Not the first time.

Perhaps the last?

As though he's reading my thoughts, David asks, "So what made you decide to live?"

I swim backwards in time, looking for the answer.

"I found a book."

I'm startled into silence.

We sit in the grass, me leaning back on my hands, David with his long legs crossed, his arms wrapped around his knees. I gaze mutely at him, absently noting his raised brows and the crinkles at the corners of his eyes. He cannot be more puzzled than I am.

"It was in a box of used books. Mom bought them. At an estate sale." I'm filling in what I know, reaching for what I cannot remember.

"There was a line in it, well that's all the book is, just a line or two on each page. But one page said…"

Frustration rises like bile. Why can't I see that page? I've turned to every page *in* that book over the last month. How could I have missed it?

"Power." I startle myself. The word comes through my lips with a life of its own, not from my conscious mind, but from a place as deep as the mermaid's home.

"Power," I say it again, wonderingly. "I can't remember *exactly*, but it said something about power.

"When I read it, I realized that if I chose to die because no one valued me enough to protect me, or loved me enough to comfort me, I gave *them* all the power.

"I realized that I had the power to choose. I could let their decisions and their actions turn my life into something worthless, or I could choose to live in a way that had meaning to me. And I realized that, if I chose to live in a way that was meaningful to me, there was always hope that it would mean something to someone else."

Ever so faintly, I hear a husky voice say, "You can make another choice."

"That's a lot of realizing." David's light tenor is softer than usual. "You realized all that when you were fourteen. Yet today, you nearly made another choice. How do we make sure you never surrender your power again?"

The "we" tugs at me, the pull is frighteningly tempting.

"It isn't a 'we' kind of problem." I'm ashamed of the sharpness in my tone. "*I'm* the one who needs to get past this. I need to do some more 'realizing.' I need to realize that I've been lying to myself. My father abused me, and I need to accept that. My mother allowed it, and I need to accept that too. In fact, everyone allowed it. I need to accept that and to accept that it wasn't *necessarily* because they didn't care."

I soften my tone, "David, I appreciate your listening. I appreciate that you care and want to help. I'm glad you don't cry for me, and hopefully don't judge me. But my history is something *I* have to come to terms with.

"Maybe someday I'll be able to share the story without being afraid of what people will think. Maybe *that* will help me to not give up that power again. If so, then you *are* helping. But to never surrender my power again, I have to come to terms with my story, and that is up to me."

A deep sadness settles over me. I am encased in a bubble of it, sadness inside me, sadness around me. Colors are muted, the sun is dimmer, David's voice comes from far, far away. I'm alone in my bubble of pathetic determination to come to terms with a tragedy that can never be undone.

"*Your* story? Dixie, what is *your* story?" I hear him. Distant though his voice may be, it reaches me in my bubble.

It plays for me, my story. Dream after dream, movies watched during soft spring nights. Story, memory, dream. But how much of it is true?

"Truth." I answer. "*My* story has to be the truth."

How loudly must I speak for him to hear me? He is so still I begin to think my words must have gotten trapped on my side of the bubble wall.

"The *truth*?" He asks finally. "What is your truth?"

Now I am the one to sit without speaking. I hear my breath, loud inside the bubble. I hear the sounds of joggers, birds and squirrels, muffled and dim.

Truth. *The* truth. *My* truth. How can they be different?

Finally, I sigh. I say to myself, softly, knowing he might hear, knowing he might not. "I've been telling *my* truth. Now it's time to face *the* truth. I was abused. It happened. I did not want to be just another victim. So, I lied to myself. I lied to everyone else. I'm not alive because I am strong. I'm not alive because I am powerful. I am alive, simply because I haven't figured out how to die."

I see it again, the flash of yellow. I hear the hum of the finely tuned engine as it shifts gears. I feel my heart's gears shifting too, slowing, my feet following suit. I see the bumper connecting with my legs, see my body cartwheeling onto the hood, through the windshield, loose and easy, no resistance.

My bubble shrinks around me, the sound of glass breaking a distant reality. The sting as it slices my face, my throat, my arms, my legs, also mercifully numbed. There in my shrinking bubble I no longer hear, no longer see, no longer feel, no longer am – anything.

The bubble bursts. What might have been the bright white light of the bridge to whatever-comes-next becomes the golden glare of summer sun. High overhead, moved out of reach of the ginkgo's sheltering branches, it slants down at my upturned face like a search light.

David is moving, legs unfolding, slow motion standing, arms reaching. I pull myself back to here-now time and focus on his face. He stops.

"Come here." It isn't a request.

He turns without waiting to see if I will obey, steps over to the flower bed, and bends over the large rose bush that anchors the curve where the bed flows past the bench like a river past a sand bar.

I go on all fours, crawling like a child. It's a short distance, but I don't trust my legs to carry me there. Even crawling takes a lifetime. He kneels next to me.

"What do you see?"

"The same thing I saw from over there. A flower garden, a rose bush, baby's breath," I take a breath to go on.

"Lean closer." He demonstrates.

I lean in, nearly topple. He steadies me, one large, capable hand on each of my shoulders.

"Now," he commands. I lean closer.

"What do you see now?"

My nose is nearly in one of the lush blossoms, everything beyond the whirl of petals is blurred and indistinct.

"A rose?" I hazard, baffled. "All I can see clearly is the rose."

"Yes," he agrees. "That is all you can see clearly."

He places his hands gently on each side of my face and moves my head to the right. "And now?" He demands. "What can you see clearly now?"

I'm looking at a thick cane jutting up through the center of the bush. It's dark, black-red with age, and sports wicked curved barbs all along its length.

Before I can answer, David's hand cups the back of my head, pushing me closer to the bush. I put my hands on the ground in front of me to keep from toppling over, swallowing the panic that swells up at the thought of falling, face first, into that wall of thorns.

Against my will, I think of what those barbs would do if I were to fall. The jagged tears they would leave on my cheeks, chin and forehead. The way the canes would snatch at my hair and clothes. I might even lose an eye if I fall forward now.

I'm trembling, partly from the effort of holding my aching body steady, partly from the imagined vision of my face being shredded by the tiny scimitars that dominate my view.

"Thorns," I admit to him. "All I can see are canes covered with thorns." I remember his lesson in rose anatomy. "Prickles, okay they're prickles. But that's all I can see."

I'm hoping he'll let me go, hoping even more that he won't. Without his long fingers to push my head back against, I think I'll have to fall either forward or back.

His hand moves away from my head, but he steadies me with his other hand, so I don't fall. He helps me to my feet, and I meet his eyes.

"Come with me." I follow meekly, noting that I don't bristle at his imperative the way I would with most people.

He moves slowly, accommodating my shorter legs and painful progress. His basket of tools and newly acquired weeds dangles from one hand, the other he holds ready to steady me if I stumble.

I make my way over the short cut grass to the sidewalk. Walking beside him, I'm aware of his height, at least a foot taller than my five foot four. He doesn't *need* to be a climbing rose to see things from a different perspective than I do. Suddenly, I realize what he'd been trying to show me, down on our knees at the edge of the rose bed.

Perspective.

What in words might be a tired cliché, a meaningless platitude, becomes a powerful illustration when your face is inches away from a velvet bloom or slashing thorns.

I remember a billboard, seen from the restaurant window where Tom and I had stopped for a bite of lunch and another review of the classifieds on a house hunting trip to St. Louis, a month or more before we moved here. I don't remember the company or organization whose name was on the sign, but I can still see the billboard itself.

Life is like a camera. Whatever you focus on is what you will develop.

That was all, or all I remember. But I never forgot those words. "Whatever you focus on is what you will develop."

That, I realized, was what David was forcing me to see. From a distance, you see a rose bush. Big picture. No particular focus. But up close, you see only what you choose to see; the rose or the thorns.

I wondered where in my story he thought I should see the rose.

We've reached the street that borders the west side of the park. He catches my arm to keep me from crossing until two oncoming cars have passed. I breathe a little chuckle that is also a sigh of relief. I *hadn't* been about to walk out in front of them, but it feels good not to *have* to pay attention, just to know someone's looking out for me right now.

We cross the street, and I realize with a start that he's headed for the brick mansion on the opposite corner. I've admired this home many times on my walks. Its fanciful turrets, arched windows, and wrought iron balconies suggest an English architect who spent time at the Pasha's court.

The porch that curls around one side of the house is deep in the shadow of a sugar magnolia, petals blushing like a spring sunrise. In this neighborhood of imposing Italianate and proper Victorian homes, this one is delightfully out of place and unforgettable.

He rings the bell while I try not to gape at the patterns in the frosted glass of the overlarge front door. Up close, I can see that the curlicues are actually leafy ferns with naked nymphs in various poses half hidden behind the fronds. The nymphs laugh at my astonishment, and I catch a glimpse of David's wry, lopsided grin as he looks down at my face.

Before I can comment, the door opens, the nymphs swinging away from view to reveal a tall, slim figure and a tired smile.

"David!" She's clearly delighted to see him. "I just put the kettle on for tea and there is a brand-new box of chocolates for you to raid!"

Her eyes drop to me. She isn't much shorter than David's six foot plus, so her eyes met his without registering my presence. Now that she has noticed me, she is suddenly awkward.

"I'm so sorry, I didn't realize…" Her voice trails away and she looks to him to save her.

"Alice," his voice is gentle as always, but with a note of formality. "I want you to meet a new friend. She's a Rose from way back, comes from many generations of Roses, we believe. Her name is Dixie. Dixie, this is Alice."

I offer a hand and she takes it, beckoning us inside. It feels like being taken under his protection, his naming me a Rose.

"Well, Dixie Rose," she says, as we follow her through a formal foyer and down a hall with wide arches framing rooms of rich furniture and low hanging chandeliers. "Do you drink tea? Or would you rather have coffee? I apologize, we don't drink soda, but I could make some iced tea if you'd rather."

"Goodness no," I assure her. "Hot tea is wonderful." I find that to be true: hot tea sounds like the perfect antidote for my ordeal just as this sense of being cared for, protected even, is the perfect antidote for the lingering memory of my dream.

We arrive in a kitchen more modern than the rooms I'd glimpsed so far, and full of light. My eye is immediately drawn to the view out of the western wall, which, except for the short run of cabinets before they turn to create a work island and bar-height seating area, is almost entirely floor to ceiling windows broken only by a set of glass paned French doors.

I realize this property must run the entire depth of this block; I'm looking into a backyard bordered by high privacy fencing with wrought iron trellises set at intervals on all three sides. On the trellises are roses. Roses riot up arches that span slate-paved walkways and sprawl in beds that curve away from the fence like gentle waves. Of course, roses aren't the only things growing. I spot iris and morning glories, hydrangeas and lilies, a regal maple and a dainty cherry still in bloom. But the roses rule this little kingdom, the rest are pale courtiers by contrast.

The conversation has gone on without me. Alice is smiling at my bemused expression. "David is the magician," she tells me. "Glenn and I have always loved roses, but until David took over, they were never very happy here. Now, as you can see," she nods and waves a hand toward the kaleidoscope of color showing through the glass, "now they're not only happy, they're joyous."

She offers me a steaming mug. I take it in both hands, holding it up to my face and letting the heat and sweet scent of apples and cinnamon work their magic on my lingering headache.

David pulls back one of the barstools and perches, heels hooked over the lowest rung of the stool to keep his long legs in check. He takes the lid off of the box of fancy chocolates Alice hands him, and offers it around. I decline, then, as he pushes it toward me again, choose a dark rectangle. Alice pops a truffle into her mouth with a sigh of pleasure and David chooses a milk chocolate in the shape of a fan.

Alice waves me to a seat in silence and, when I've settled myself at the bar, she leans down to rest her elbows on the worktop, standing slack-hipped like a resting horse, her hands wrapped around her mug, her gaze unfocused on something not in the room.

"How is Glenn?" David's voice startles Alice and I both. He reaches for another chocolate. His third, I think. We were all lost in private thoughts when he consumed his second.

Alice turns her head to meet his eyes, and I see her in profile. Hard to guess her age, I've never been good at that anyway. She might be 50, she might be closer to 60. Her hair still shows the auburn it once was, but it's mostly faded to a peachy gray, and it could use a trim. The cut is modern, though, a shingled bob of baby-fine wisps layered close to her finely shaped scalp.

Whatever her age, she looks tired. Those dark circles under her eyes aren't a sign of years, but of no sleep and worry. A dusting of pale freckles against the papery white skin suggests it has been a long time since she's spent time in the sun and the open air.

She's built to be all softened angles, with the willowy, graceful lines I admire but could never aspire to have. Those hollowed cheeks aren't fashion or genetics, however, and neither is the pinched look of her thin lips.

This is a woman who has nearly reached her limit. I recognize the signs.

She sighs deeply before she answers.

"He's better today. I'm sure he'd love to see you. And meet your new Rose."

"Good." David's voice is decisive. He snags another chocolate from the box and unfolds his legs to get to his feet. I notice that all the milk chocolate choices are gone, only truffles and dark chocolates remain. A rose that thrives on chocolate, who would ever believe it?

David gives me a look clearly intended as, "Come with me." I get to my feet as well, but decline the offer of the box of chocolates pushed in my direction. He shrugs – a silent, "Suit yourself, but I don't understand."

Alice leads us down the wide hall, my running shoes squeaking a little on the polished wood floor, David's moccasins, as usual, making not a sound. Alice is barefoot. I find that deeply endearing, her welcoming us into her elegant home in bare feet.

She turns into a large room. The sunlight here is filtered through heavy woven drapes of silvery blue. If opened, the windows would look out on the same view that I had seen through the kitchen windows.

The room was probably designed as an office. Our feet sink into deep pile carpet the color of soft charcoal, the walls are papered in a woven texture that only misses being masculine by the metallic glint of silver threaded through the weave. But it doesn't take the hospital bed in front of the window to tell me that this is now a sick room – there is a quality to the air, unmistakable to anyone who has ever cared for a bedridden patient, that marks a place where someone spends days and nights in view of death.

The man propped against the pillows has his face turned toward the window. He turns toward us before slowly opening his eyes. I first notice the clear tubing of the oxygen cannula, belatedly registering the canister by the bed and the faint hiss of the open valve.

My focus shifts as his eyes open, their piercing blue so compelling it drives other observations to the background. They fix first on Alice and David, I feel it the instant he notices me, standing awkwardly a little behind them.

It is David who moves forward, bending over the bed and resting a hand on the thin shoulder as he smooths the navy lapel of the pajama top. "Glenn," he beckons me closer as he speaks. "I want to introduce you to an old friend I just met. She's had a bit of a rough day, but I think you two might have a lot to share."

I move to stand beside him, my head barely reaching his shoulder. I don't know if I should offer to shake hands with the frail figure in the bed, but I smile as warmly as I can into those ice-blue eyes.

He settles my unspoken question by reaching out his hand. His wrist is thin, but his grip is strong and business-like. His smile is as warm as mine feels and, when it reaches his eyes, they go from ice to the sparkle of a mountain lake.

"So, *you're* David's discovery. He mentioned he'd met a Rose in the garden. Alice and I hoped he'd bring you along for a visit."

I stammer something that I hope is appropriate, certain that David has a reason for putting us together, baffled as to what that reason might be.

"David," Glenn's voice is reedy thin, but clearly used to command, "why don't you pull up a chair for your Rose? You and Alice are tired of my stories. It will be nice to have a new audience."

David positions a club chair near the bed and uses the buttons on the footboard to lower the height of the mattress and lift the head of the bed so that Glenn can easily see me where I'm sitting in the chair. I settle back, the firm cushions and luxurious velvet weave of the chair receiving my body weight like they were custom made for me.

"Where shall we begin?" Glenn asks after David and Alice have excused themselves, Alice to the waiting lunch dishes and David to the garden.

He answers his own question. "Perhaps you might tell me what you do with yourself when you aren't playing in David's rose beds."

So, I tell him a little of my work. It feels trivial to talk of business mergers and management systems, of team dynamics and client advocacy, but trivial is a wonderful contrast to the drama of my memories.

Glenn meets my tales with stories of his own. He's been in business most of his life, he says, and team dynamics are, or were, his specialty.

We swap stories until Alice reappears with a glass of juice in one hand and a dish of capsules and tablets in the other.

"I'm so sorry to interrupt you two," she begins. "But Glenn needs to get these meds down before three o'clock."

Startled, I realize we've been chatting for nearly two hours. Glenn's voice still sounds strong, but surely he isn't supposed to be this animated for so long. I get to my feet, having to steady myself on the bed rail as my legs receive my weight.

Glenn pauses with the glass halfway to his mouth and raises an eyebrow at me. I wink, trying to match his easy manners. "That chair was just too comfortable," I pass off his concern. "My legs tried to go to sleep without me."

His eyes take in my hand, still gripping the bed rail, white-knuckled. I'm sure the strain shows in my face as well; I can feel the muscles around my left eye twitching. But he nods and gulps down the juice, chasing the handful of pills.

He hands the juice glass back to Alice and holds out his hand. I take it and he places his left over the top of mine. "I understand now why David wanted us to meet; please visit when you can."

I thank him for the stories, assure him that I'd love to come again, and turn to find David standing in the doorway. Next to him is a slim, straight figure in flame red cotton. I'm not sure which of them I am happier to see.

As we leave the room, the child walks in front, David and I following, and Alice coming behind us into the kitchen. It is flooded in light now, the afternoon sun angling in that western wall of glass so that we have to squint to look outside, making the garden beyond look like an impressionistic painting.

David and I say goodbye to Alice. The child settles onto one of the bar stools, quite at home. She meets my eyes calmly, almost challengingly, as she reaches for the box of chocolates and chooses a truffle so dark it is nearly black. My breath refuses to leave my body as I watch her place it on her tongue, then chew and swallow.

So much for thinking she doesn't need sugar.

David gives one last wave. I don't know if it is only for Alice, or if he too can see the slim figure at the bar.

We walk slowly back through the park. I'd like to ask him, was he waving at one friend, or two? But I don't want to break the companionable silence. He paces me all the way to my car and waits until I've pulled my keys from my pocket.

"Thank you." I want to say so much more, but those are the only words I can form that make sense.

He nods solemnly, not speaking. I have to stand on tiptoe to hug him, and lifting my arms to reach around his neck hurts the whole length of me. It catches him off guard, and he returns the hug only gingerly, but I can tell it pleases him and his eyes are twinkling when he says, "Be careful with yourself, Dixie Rose. I expect to see you back here in one piece and soon."

I nod my acceptance of his expectation and slide behind the wheel.

JUNE

For the Flint Hills, in the center of Kansas, a place few Americans know about and even fewer have visited, June is a month of rampant growth, green and gold spreading over the gray and brown of the earth and rocks. As though Mother Earth is anxious that her country child not be discovered naked and bare on the Solstice.

I'd come early to the little town of McPherson. Snuck in without telling Milt and Toni, dumped my bags at the hotel and driven back to the stone fortress on the hill that I have begun to think of as "my castle." The place where I first thought I saw the rider in the flesh, the girl I had dubbed the "warrior child," who revealed herself as the spirit sister of my dreams.

I had taken her then for my private hallucination, the girl and her horse symbolizing for me a strength and freedom I'd lost on my twisted path to here and now. Just as I was learning to enjoy the reality of her, as I had begun to remember a time when she had been a natural part of my life, I'd come up against a past-turned-present in which I had sent her away.

I sometimes see her, playing with kids in the park for all the world like a real child. Sometimes she swaps the red cotton dress for t-shirts and shorts, although she's always wearing that same shade of red. I see her with Glenn; he chats with her as though her he's known her all his life, calls her "Little Rose" and asks after her when I visit, and she isn't there. But not a word has she said to me.

So, I drive to Coronado Heights again. Coronado came then in search of a mythical kingdom made real on Earth. I come now in search of answers from a mystical spirit turned solid flesh.

I don't climb the steps this time. Don't even enter the cool stone building. Instead I take the blanket I borrowed at the hotel and place it, still folded, on a patch of clover. I sit on it, cross-legged and closed-eyed, as I would before a yoga session, meditating, facing the dying sun.

I don't open my eyes when I hear the hoof falls. I listen to them slowing, the clomp clomp of a walk, then stopping. No sound as her feet touch the ground, but I know she is coming toward me, can feel her like you feel the metal in a fork before it touches your teeth.

I open my eyes and there she is, exactly where I knew she would be. Sitting across from me, the patch of clover spread between us like an altar cloth, her horse whuffling softly at the grasses a few feet away.

I look a question at her. She answers it without clarifying my thought.

"Do you understand now? You set yourself a test, and you passed it. You didn't make it easy on him. You didn't beg him to stop, you didn't pretend to be broken. He didn't stop because he thought he'd won. He didn't stop because you threatened him or rejected him. He stopped because he found a place inside himself where he had to stop.

"When it was done, he found he'd reached the full depth of his anger and fear. He saw himself as he had become, and he made a different choice."

She is quiet. Everything said.

I pluck a handful of clover, sort through the clusters looking for one with four leaves. I replay her answer. I cannot connect it to my question.

I came here wanting to know who I am, what I am accomplishing with this life I have been given, if we really do choose our purpose and our destiny before we are born.

I came here to ask about the lines missing from my little red book. The ones that told me I had power. And that I was free to choose.

Who am I? What am I here to do? Why do I make these choices? How do I reclaim my power? *Those* were my questions.

I keep looking at my handful of clover leaves. *Just once*, I'm thinking, *just once show me a four-leaf clover.*

"I'm looking over a four-leaf clover…" The tune is unbidden and unavoidable. "That I overlooked before…" On it plays, no words now, but a tune pushing at my lips wanting to be hummed, sung, shouted.

I turn my hands over, letting the leaves fall between us, and dust my palms together in a gesture universally used to indicate "good riddance."

I'm halfway to my feet when her eyes tug at me, demanding attention. I ease back to my blanket, cross my legs, and wait. Her gaze never shifts. She says nothing.

"Okay, what did I miss?" I say. "What am I overlooking?" It doesn't occur to me she might not know the reference. Any song that plays in my mind surely plays in hers.

"How would you describe yourself? Three words."

What is this? An interview? I want to tell her I'm not qualified, I don't even want to apply for the position. But I'm curious. So, I give it some thought.

"Stubborn." I give her the first word that comes to mind.

"Passionate. Compassionate too," I add.

"Sometimes I wish I weren't so compassionate. Or stubborn. Or passionate. That gets me in a lot of trouble. It might be easier if I were less of all three, but I guess that's how I'd describe myself."

"What do you call it when you work with young horses? Not breaking them, you…" She lets it trail off, expecting me to fill in the blank.

"You gentle them."

I'm reminded of the story I'd told Bud. About the first pony that was mine.

"Like I did Trixie," I venture, remembering that she would have been there with me when I finally got the pony I'd been begging for: my Shetland mare, wild-eyed and skittish, bay coat rough and mane and tail tangled. She would have laughed too, learning that this creature had already been named Trixie, and that she, like me, was seven years old. Trixie and Dixie, wild seven-year-olds teaching each other how to trust, how to love and how to live.

"Poor thing," I'm still remembering, "she'd been so abused and neglected. She had a mouth of stone, she couldn't even feel the bit, and I was only seven. I didn't have the strength to rein her in if she decided to run. I just held on and figured wherever we ended up we'd end up there together. Usually, it was just back at the barn. But I *had* to 'gentle' her. Well, and out-stubborn her, but I finally did it."

Trixie had tested me and tested herself. I barely remember the terror and determination of clinging to her mane, knees tucked tight against her withers, riding bareback because my father didn't think I needed a saddle. But I remember *clearly* the day she let me groom her neck and stroke her ears without twitching them away.

I can see her in the pasture watching me approach, bit clutched in one small hand to warm it, reins looped over my arm. See the way she lifts her head and perks her ears, the way she ambles in my direction then abandons her causal façade and trots to me, nearly shoving her ears into the headstall.

I can hear the air blowing against her loose horsey lips, and her thought behind it, "We're going to run, yeah, we're going to run, fun, run, fun, we're going to RUN!"

"Your father," her husky voice brings me back to whatever here and now one is in when one is having a conversation with a child who has gone from figment-of-imagination to solid-takes-up-space-flattens-grasses-when-she-sits-on-them status.

"He was stubborn?"

"You're asking me?" I explode back at her. "You know good and well how stubborn he was. If he wanted something to move, it moved, if he wanted something to break, it broke, if he wanted *anything* it was going to happen."

"Mmm," a non-comment offered through closed lips. I wonder if she's picked that up from David. "Would you say he was passionate?"

"Well, he was intense. I don't know that'd I say passionate. Maybe, but he tried to keep it under control. Thought everyone else should too."

But then I'm seeing him with my mother, studying a kitchen tableful of seed catalogs and *Mother Earth News* magazines. I see their careful lists, seeds and plants they want to try, new varieties, new offerings, new challenges. I'm seeing him scooping shovelful after shovelful of cow manure, so old and dried it has no smell, spreading it in heaps over the clayish soil of what would be a lush garden.

Hearing his voice as he drives me to lift one more shovel full, push one more wheelbarrow load, scatter one more bale of rotting straw. I see him working through the dusk, tilling, turning, weeding, harvesting, until the stars and the mosquitoes came out together and make more work impossible.

"Yeah, he was passionate."

"Compassionate?"

I'd seen this challenge coming, I'd been bracing for it. "What *is* compassion anyway?" I wonder aloud.

I thumb through my mental reference books looking for a clue. Come up with second semester Latin, "passion" from the verb "pati" meaning "to suffer." I'd puzzled over that, until I thought of the expression common in old romance novels, "He suffered from a long and enduring passion."

Thinking that through now, I realize that my father had, indeed, been one of the most passionate people I'd ever known. He believed in suffering for what you wanted most and suffering until you made it a reality.

But compassionate? I parse it out. "Com" could be from the Latin "cum" meaning "with." So did compassionate literally translate as "to suffer with?" I feel my eyebrows coming together and rub at the space between them with the heel of one hand.

I had my answer.

"In his last few years, he learned compassion. Before that, he was quick to judge, especially if he didn't understand, if someone was very different from him or lived by different rules. He figured that girls who got raped were probably 'asking for it' and so were people who went to the big city and walked downtown at night. But later he developed a softer attitude, he was more accepting, more able to put himself in someone else's shoes even if he didn't have much in common with them. Yes, compassionate.

"Maybe," I theorize, "it was because he knew he was dying."

"He'd faced death before, right?" she counters. "How was he when he first knew he had cancer and could die?"

"Oh, he was angry! No, when he was fighting cancer the first time it didn't have that effect. But I saw him soften before even he knew the cancer had come back. It was after I left home, I know.

"Maybe that was it, because I was gone, I wasn't there to antagonize him or challenge him anymore." I don't like the thought, but I repeat it anyway. "Maybe that was the biggest difference."

"Or maybe it was because you kept coming back."

That suggestion drops into the patch of clover between us, and I watch the space where it falls. My eyes can't see it for tears, and it sinks in for a long moment before I look at her.

She is so slight, this stoic child. I was never so thin or so composed. She's got my strong will, I think. And the compassion. If we are twin souls, my passion has missed her completely.

"You kept coming back," she repeats. "You, who had been so glad to escape, and he knew you had good reason. Don't you think that *maybe* he expected that you would leave and never come back? That you'd despise him for what he'd done?

"Don't you think *maybe* that is why he tried to keep you needing his support, tried to convince you that you were helpless about anything mechanical, tried to paint you as impractical and unprepared to live in the world? Because *maybe* he figured, even dreaded, that once you realized your independence you would never come home again? Don't you think *maybe*?"

"But I did go back! I went often. I took care of things. I took care of *him* when he was dying. If he thought *that*, he was wrong about me!"

She is nodding. I can see I've made her point, but I'm not sure what point she and I are making together out here on the prairie with an unlikely castle to the north and a Kansas sunset blazing itself to death to the west. I came here hoping for answers. So far, she has told me my answer was a test I have already passed, then given me a test of questions that I cannot possibly answer.

Finally, she offers me the gift I came here to find.

"You showed him compassion. You loved who he was at his core. You took his anger and his fear and his need to control the world through controlling you. You stayed with him in his suffering, and you reflected it back to him as understanding and love and permission to be his best self — the self you saw and loved, beyond reason and without condition. You gave him a new truth about *himself*."

I'm looking at her, wonderstruck, hands frozen in front of me, fingers clutching the clover, unable to move them to wipe away the tears streaming down my cheeks.

"Without learning compassion, he could not 'gentle' you, he could only try to break you. But you saw it for what it was, and you took it in but did not break. You threw your will against his, almost to your death, and you thought he had won. But he didn't win. You didn't die, you didn't break, and you did not even hate him for trying.

"You saw through his anger and fear, you recognized his suffering. You transformed it, and you gave it back to him with a whole heart, a heart full of compassion such as he had never known.

"You said he learned compassion — Dixie, who do you think he learned it *from?"*

I sit in the grass long after she's gone. She'd touched me before she went. She'd risen gracefully in one flowing motion, the way I *wished* I could do, but could no longer manage, and stood perfectly still, waiting for something I couldn't guess at. At last she had moved, bending to put her hands against my wet cheeks. She'd smiled, the easiest, sweetest smile I had ever seen on her face. I think, I really do think, she winked.

Her horse came to meet her as if pulled by a string of mutual understanding. She'd vaulted lightly to his back, and they were gone.

But that startling suggestion, that miraculous explanation, stayed; playing over and over until, like the memory I'd had of my father in the garden, the stars and the mosquitoes both came out to play.

"Dixie, who do you think he learned it from?" Her gentle challenge follows me through days spent with clients and long summer evenings in the park.

I work, kneeling next to David, weeding, mulching, deadheading. He talks of rose care and lore. I listen for lessons on growing and blooming.

Other times, I sit next to Glenn's bed while he talks to me of his career, coming into one department after another to pull a team together, create the foundation of trust and common objectives needed to pull off miracles in the marketplace. I hear the passion and power still echoing in his voice, now faint enough that the hiss and flow of oxygen through the tubes can be heard plainly as an accompanying rhythm.

It makes me think about what illness would have represented to my father, a man used to moving mountains through physical force, and commanding obedience by sheer force of will, having to watch his last child escaping his control, and feel his body refusing to comply with his desires.

I think, too, about how it touched and molded me. His illness, his fear, his anger. All coming together in that one night I had allowed to redefine my life.

My spirit sister is my constant companion during the evening time after dinner when Tom is watching golf or movies and I'm sitting with my red book and my journal. She kneels silent in the grass with David and me when we're weeding, or perches at the foot of Glenn's hospital bed, listening intently to the stories, or perhaps listening between the lines for truths we do not intend to share. When I rise from my yoga mat and walk to the park to meet Vincent, I find her waiting for me on a park bench, or with the kids and dogs that romp over the grassy spaces between paths and flower beds.

I forget about pain, seldom noticing even the faintest twinge. The vivid dream fades into a mistier memory than that time has ever been in my mind. The details that have been so sharp for years fade, leaving room for nuances I've never noticed.

I let thoughts flow in the birdsong-broken, easy silence that David and I share, or let my mind wander while Vincent's cheerful voice sets a pace for our walks.

To the rhythm of one-foot-in-front-of-another or tug-drop-into-basket-reach-for-the-next-weed, I hammer out my truth about that night and my life before and after.

Before that night I'd seen my father and I as equal combatants. His will against mine. His anger and punishment against my stubbornness and ability to endure. And I was winning. I could not be broken; I would *not* concede.

So, if I was winning, why did I secretly hope someone would stop him? I'd hoped that someone would notice the welts and bruises and take my side. Not because I needed saving, but because I wanted validation. I wanted someone to confirm what I hoped was true; he was not right to beat me, I was not deserving of such treatment.

I'd felt alone. But I'd also felt strong, a worthy opponent for him regardless of the difference in size, or age, or position.

Till one day the rhythm is broken by a flash of truth so startling that I hold my breath in stunned non-motion, taking it in.

It wasn't the beating of my body that I feared, but the besting of my will. Until that night, whenever the switch or the belt or the fist fell, I'd held up my stoicism as superiority. I would *not* break.

But that night my superiority failed me. I saw myself, no more than a frightened animal, screaming in pain and terror. The only armor I'd ever had, my will and determination to endure his unfair punishments without crying or begging for it to end, that armor had been stripped away. I was naked. I was defenseless. I could not win.

I leave the park with only a sketch of a wave to David. The girl follows me to the car, but, once there, she gives me a quick hug and vanishes. This thread is mine to untangle. On my own.

That night I add another complete poem to my journal.

When it is finished, I hand it to the still figure of the girl who suddenly appears to be curled in the other chair in front of the dead fireplace. Without comment, I hug her and leave her to read it alone while I go off to bed.

The words I'd written play in my head, but I don't dream.

The next day is Saturday. Yoga class is over. I'm listening to Vincent talk about his last match, stretching myself to keep up with his strides and animated stories, when my thoughts veer off on another path entirely.

A memory of my brother's voice overlaps Vincent's voice in my ear.

"We had this old milk cow," he'd begun. "And she kicked and wouldn't let down milk. And one day Dad just lost it and started beating her. I held out as long as I could, then I said, 'Dad, if you're gonna kill her anyway, why don't I just get the gun?'"

What unleashed his anger, I wonder? What was so overpowering that he risked killing the cow, and later, me, because he couldn't control his temper?

I replay the scene, the dream superimposed over memory, making sounds of agreement when Vincent's patter leaves a quiet space, waiting for an answer to come to me.

I see myself stumbling backward, away from the striking hand, toward the hot cast iron. I feel the terror clawing its way out of my mouth, the scream cut short as I make the desperate slide for the corner and freedom.

The answer comes. So abruptly that I stop. Vincent retraces his steps to come back to my side. I can barely see him, barely move to shake my head at his question.

Whatever the question, the answer is "No."

No, I don't want to sit down. No, I'm not sick. No, I'm not all right. Just no.

I root myself to the sidewalk and let understanding rush through me – sap pouring into a plant seen in time lapse photography.

Vincent's hands are on my shoulders, he's shaking me gently, forward and back, while my head shakes from side to side. The answer is still just "no."

In the wash of understanding, I see the irony. What if, for my father *and* myself, what caused us *both* to lose control of our temper was the *fear* of giving up control?

We were the same.

She was right, the warrior child, when she said we had engaged in a battle of wills. We were battling for control. Control of what? What was worth such fear? Such rage? Such risk?

Of me. We battled for control of *me*!

I look up at Vincent's frightened face and nod.

"I need coffee." I'm already turning toward the café, and he follows without a word.

Hands wrapped around a frothy latte, I tell Vincent the tale.

Recounting it for David, the aftermath of the dream amplified by bruises gotten in my encounter with the yellow sports car, I'd flinched away from tender places and clenched my teeth in others.

This telling is easy. Almost, in this version, I confuse my father with myself, so alike do I realize we were. It's almost funny to think of us, after years of being locked in a battle of wills, finally making the battle real. And nearly final.

That's sobering. I look up from what is left in my cup. "I know I could have died, could have fractured my skull instead of my nose. Could have broken a vein instead of capillaries. But I'm hard to kill."

I flinch away from that too, remembering how near I'd come to doing just that.

"And if I could have reached that poker…" my voice fades as I wonder what exactly I might have been capable of doing. Yes, it could have ended much differently.

Vincent's outburst is so fierce and unexpected I nearly spill the last of my latte.

"I wish you *had* gotten your hands on that poker! I wish you had shown that bastard exactly what you were made of! I can *not* believe he got away with that shit, and *no one* did anything!"

"Well," I admit, "that was the hardest for me. I guess it still is. Not that he got away with it, but that all the people I thought were my friends, my family, the adults in my life who cared for me and were responsible for my well-being, those people didn't do a thing. They pretended not to even see."

His anger is still overflowing. "Well, let me tell you what *I* would have done! I'd have made sure that man never lifted his hand to anyone ever again except the other assholes serving time with him. I'd have beat *his* head against a wall first, just to see how he liked it. I'd have…" I'm thankful that he's run out of imagination. Or just out of breath.

"That is my father you're talking about," I remind him. "A man I love and still miss very much."

Vincent shakes his head so hard his dreadlocks flop about his face. "He was your father. You might think you *have* to love him, and you're a good person for forgiving him and everyone else, but there is *no* excuse for that. Not for him, not for your mother, not for your teachers, not for all those other pantywaist freakshows that didn't do what any decent person would have done!"

I hold up a hand. I'd like to push his words back into his mouth, pretend that those thoughts had never crossed his mind. Or mine.

But he's only echoing what *I* once thought. I too, had gotten lost in the dark labyrinth of judgment and reason. I'd vacillated between demanding retribution and condemning myself to a life of worthlessness because no one thought me worth protecting. Back and forth I'd gone, hating them, hating me, until I concluded that my life just didn't matter. Not to anyone.

Judgment and reason said they didn't lift a finger to help me because I wasn't worth the effort. They didn't worry about the next time my father lost his temper, just like they hadn't worried about the next time any *other* time he lost his temper. And surely they knew that one of those next times, I could end up dead.

Judgment and reason had come closer to getting me killed than my father's rage had ever come.

But I'm not lost in that labyrinth anymore.

"Vincent. . . . Vincent." I have to say his name twice to get him to look at me. He's staring into the far distance as though he might be able to identify the enemy and defeat him even now.

"Vincent, they aren't . . . They weren't . . ." He brings his focus back to my face and I begin again.

"People aren't monsters." My voice is flat and tight, my hand grips the handle of the latte mug so tightly I'm surprised it doesn't shatter. "They were not bad people."

I soften my voice, it's effort, but I want him to hear me. *I* want to hear me.

"Are all the people you meet good and innocent? You say there are lots of good people out there, and you thank God for introducing you to them. But how do you know that all those good people you meet haven't done what my father did? What my mother did? What all those people in the community did, or didn't do?

"Are *you* so good and innocent? Can you really say you've never abused anyone or let someone be abused?"

He flares at that. "I've never, ever hit a child, or *anyone* except in the ring or in selfdefense! And if I *ever* saw a child with bruises like that, I wouldn't just ignore them!"

He takes a breath to go on, but I hold up a hand again to stop him.

"Is that your only definition for abuse?" I challenge him. "Bruises? Well, let me tell you that was the least of it. Except for that one time, when I really thought I might die, I'd rather take a beating than be mocked, or put down, or belittled. I'd rather have had him hit me with anything he could find, than listen to him saying, 'You don't know what *work* really is," one more time.

Abuse takes a lot of forms, my friend, and I'll bet you've been guilty of one of them."

He'd like to interrupt, but I'm not finished. "Are you going to tell me you've never gone off on someone weaker than you, or someone who couldn't defend themselves? Never gotten all pissed off because you ordered a hamburger and got a chicken sandwich? Or because your food took too long coming and you were *starving*? Isn't that abuse?

"Do you think you're the perfect white knight? You've never seen someone else being berated and stood silent? Never watched a kid getting picked on and gone on about your business? I'll bet you have, at least once."

I hold up my hand once more as he takes a breath to speak.

"Yeah, I know. You've never done anything '*that bad.*' But don't you see, it's all just degrees. We've all been the abuser and we've all been the observer who did nothing at all."

"I don't see how you can say that." He's gone from angry to bewildered, but his head still shakes back and forth, just as mine had standing on the sidewalk awash in understanding that my father and I were the same.

"You're a victim of something a *lot* more damaging than just getting dressed down because someone didn't do their job. It doesn't even compare. That stuff happens, it's no big deal. But what they did to *you* is a crime!"

"I am *not* a victim!" I spit it out so fast my words overlap his own.

He waves a long-fingered hand. "Victim, survivor, whatever you want. What they did to you was *wrong*! Someday you're going to look back and realize you need closure, you need someone to blame, someone to face the music, and all that pain and anger you think you're so *over* is going to come back and bite you in the ass."

"Oh, you think so? You think I need to blame someone? Where do you suggest I begin? With my father? Well, *his* father used a bullwhip on him. And when *he* was growing up no one considered that *abuse*. Back then, children were property; parents had the right to do anything they wanted to them. Shall I blame my ancestors for believing what their culture taught him to believe? Shall I blame all of society? How wide and how deep do you want me to throw that net of blame?

"I don't care what you call me, I'm no different than anyone else. Sure, I'm a survivor. Aren't we all survivors? We've *all* survived something. Lots of things. Pleasant things. Painful things. Stupid things. I'm doing *more* than surviving, I'm *living!*

"I guess you could say I've *been* a victim. We've all been victims. Of something. I'm sure you've been a victim of racism. Does that make you a victim, as a person? Is that how you identify yourself? *You* could walk around being a victim, all geared up for the next attack, but you don't and I'm not going to. I *refuse* to be a victim, no matter *who* does *what* to me.

"Being victimized is a situation, an event. *Being* a victim is a *choice.* I've been in that situation, but I am *not* going to make that choice."

I'm drained. My emotion has washed through me like a sudden rainstorm through a dry gully – running in spate, leaving behind only traces of mud.

We sit in uneasy silence. He wanders to the counter to add hot coffee to the cold milk that remains in his cup. When he returns to our table he's carrying a basket with two chocolate croissants – a break in training for him.

I want something hot; the June sun outside isn't keeping the chill from my fingers in here. I go to the counter and order a hot tea. The barista raises her eyebrows at my emphasis on "hot," but she fills a big mug with water just short of boiling and holds out the tea caddy with an invitation to "pick my poison." I choose a triangular net bag labeled "soothing pear and cinnamon" and return to where Vincent is staring out the window at the park drowsing in sun and shade.

He's finished off one of the croissants; he pushes the basket my way. While my tea steeps, I pull the croissant into flaky bites, savoring every one as the buttery pastry dissolves on my tongue, releasing a core of rich, dark chocolate.

Growing up, I read about croissants. They were what sophisticated people ate for breakfast, off trays presented by deferential servants, while they themselves lounged in bed or sat in their dressing gowns on balconies high above formal gardens.

My, I *have* come a long, long way. No servants in livery. No high balconies. But here I am, lounging with my tea and croissants, looking out at gorgeous gardens with a friend who at least cares enough for me to be battle ready over something that happened many years ago.

I feel the slow smile spreading over my face. I can even feel the little crinkle in my nose that only happens when I'm particularly delighted. Vincent turns toward me like a man who's just become aware of the sun's emergence from behind a cloud.

"What?" He demands. "What's that silly grin about?"

"Do you remember our first walk? You said you felt like God has given you so much?"

"I remember our walk. I don't remember what I said. Why?"

"Because I know exactly what you mean, how blessed you feel. And I want to thank you for helping me feel it."

"What? You feel blessed? You've just been telling me this story about how you got beat up, damned near *killed*, by your dad, and suddenly you feel blessed? You wanna explain that to me?"

I *do*. I *do* want to explain it to him. I *want* to include him in this dazzling truth of present understanding.

"Look at me, Vincent. Forget what you *think* happened to me and think about my life *now*. I couldn't be further from that girl who wanted to die because she believed she had no worth. Why, so many people value my time, I barely *have* time for all of them. And I want to spend as much time with them as I can, because they make *me* feel good!

"Do you think those people would be in my life, would *you* be in my life, if I weren't *me*? Think about our first walk together. You said you wanted to walk with me because I had good energy. You said I had a 'light thing' going. I thought you were hitting on me, almost told you where to go, but I'm glad I was wrong."

Now it's his turn for a slow smile. "Oh, you weren't wrong. I was. But you're too much for me to handle. I decided I'd have to settle for being 'just friends.'"

I have to laugh. Too much for him to handle indeed. Well, perhaps he has a point.

"Okay, I'll take that as a compliment. But, you wouldn't have *wanted* to walk with me if I'd been 'just another pretty girl.' You see pretty girls in the park every day. Girls that are *way* prettier than I *ever* was, even when I was prettier.

Girls that could pace you on a training run instead of having to work hard to keep up with your fast walk. Girls that are your age, with perfect skin and buns. And you don't even glance at them when you're walking with me.

"And you *keep* walking with me. You walk with me, you have coffee with me, you talk to me, and you get way bent-out-of-shape-protective of me over something that is ancient history. That isn't about you thinking I'm pretty, or even sexy, it's not because you think you're going to 'get some' or because you fancy yourself in love with me. That's about me being me and you liking to be with me because I *am* me. Am I right?"

"Yeah, of course you're right." He hasn't seen it yet, this gift that *I* am just now unwrapping.

"Who would I be if my life had been different?" I toss the challenge down and sit back to wait for his response.

It's a long time coming. I can't tell what is going on behind his dark hazel-flecked eyes. They examine my face, a little line forming between them as he ponders.

"You'd still be you," he asserts. "You'd be different, but you'd still be you."

"Okay, I'd be me. But I wouldn't be *this* version of me. I might be a version you wouldn't like to spend time with at all. I might be a version you'd fall head over heels for. I don't know what *that* me would be, but it wouldn't be this one.

"That's the *truth*, Vincent.

"*We become who we are by living.* If my life had been different, *I* would be different. I choose who I become by choosing my life, and I choose my life by choosing who I become."

"But you didn't." He's still puzzled. "You didn't choose *that*. Who would? I can see you're stronger for it. And maybe forgiving your dad and mom and all those other people has made you a better person, but you didn't choose that."

"You don't think so?" A little laugh escapes me as I hear a husky voice repeat, "You're having a reaction, Little One, and you can choose."

"*I* think I did. I think I *did* choose to go through the 'fire' so to speak. I think I chose it the same way you choose to train, the same way you choose to spar, the same way you choose your practice matches. I chose to hone my *self.* I chose to become a powerhouse in what you might call the 'ring of life.'

"I chose my trials so I could choose my battles. And win!"

Silently, I add a resounding "SO THERE!" to all the people who might pity me, thinking of me as just another victim. I add a belated "THANK YOU" to the people who looked away from the girl hiding a battered face behind waves of chestnut hair, leaving her to find her own way into power, to take her place in that ring, ready for anything. I even add a love song for the woman that girl has become.

For me.

"Every true story has, at its heart, a homeward path, a key to the maze, a map that shows where we begin, and where we belong."

And on the opposing page:

Never change your true story, for only your truth can provide the compass and the power to find your way back home.

So says my little red book when I pull it from my bag and let it fall open.

I'd left Vincent without easing his mind. I could feel the new distance between us as he gave me his customary goodbye hug. I've pushed the previously known limits of his understanding too far for him to adjust. He's off balance with me.

That's okay, I think, sitting in the sunhot car with the little book propped against the steering wheel. I've been pushing the known boundaries of my understanding too. And I get off balance with me sometimes. But each time, I've rediscovered balance, and each time I'm stronger, more agile, more flexible, more *sure* than I was before.

I let my eyes fall on the open pages. Perhaps I am finding my balance through finding my truth. My story. My *true* story. The one that has the power to guide me home.

I'd come back through the park slowly, eyes restless, feet reluctant. I realized I was looking for David, not consciously, but with that instinctive need to test a theory, share a discovery, with someone you trust to reflect truth back to you honestly and without judgment.

So I meandered the park paths, glancing at each tidy bed of blooms, expecting to see his long frame folded into itself as he clipped or pulled the bits that did not belong. Finally, my feet brought me to the curb where my car sat waiting and I pulled my keys out of my pocket and slid into the driver's seat.

I hear his question again, "What are we going to do to make sure you don't relinquish that power again?"

I'd told him then it wasn't a "we" kind of problem. I remembered, too, that moment of temptation. The longing to be not-alone.

Like a sliver of sun lifting itself over an illusionary mountain, I see that it *is* a "we" kind of problem.

It is always a "we" kind of problem because *no one* solves that problem alone. The truth of our story is tested against mirror after mirror. Our power is tested in trial after trial. The analogy I'd offered Vincent before our goodbye hug comes back to me: No boxer has ever won a bout by practicing *only* against the bag.

What beautiful clarity Vincent has offered me, walk after walk together, chattering blithely on about his sport, the trainers and coaches he'd worked with, the bouts he won and lost, the sparring partners and opponents in the ring.

Before meeting Vincent, I'd known nothing of boxing. I'd never been aware of the vast number of people it takes to make one boxer successful. We see only the match, the boxer alone in the ring with his opponent and the coach, squirting water in the general direction of the boxer's face, wiping away sweat and blood, sending the lone warrior back into combat with a few last admonishments and words of encouragement.

From Vincent, I've learned of all the other roles in his boxing life. He has a fitness trainer who oversees his workout schedule, he has two boxing coaches, plus a team of other boxers who spar with him and join his friends and family to cheer him on when he competes.

He has practice opponents who come into the ring with him, knowing they're there to be outclassed. And he has practice rounds with opponents who far outclass him, from whom he learns subtleties that can only be learned in the ring. Finally, he has the opponents he meets in his official bouts.

I'd told him I believed I'd chosen my challenges in order to have the power to win in the "ring of life." I'd seen my opponents, finally learned to accept the gifts they offered. But what about the coaches, the trainers, the team members and the cheerleaders who've offered themselves through the years? Why had I thought my power more precious if I believed I'd gained it alone?

"The compass and the power to find my way back home." If I tell my story true, my life has been peopled by as many coaches, trainers, teammates, and cheerleaders as it has by opponents. If I tell my story true, I have never been alone at all.

A warm sense of peace and power washes over me, wraps me in spirals of happy knowing: I am never alone.

Sure enough, I'm not. The slim figure in the passenger seat calmly reaches over her shoulder for the seat belt. Turning back to fasten it securely, she winks and smiles.

JULY

Summer comes in full gypsy dress. The roses show off every color from gaudy red, yellow, and orange to shy blush and creamy white.

Children display bare bronzed shoulders touched with ruddy sunburn left over from a day at the pool, and joggers and moseyers alike bare as much skin as they dare. Serious athletes, and some not-so-serious, run in sports bras, or, for the men, in no shirt at all.

Even Alice, when I coax her out for a walk with me, chooses a purple tank top and blue jean shorts.

David comes to the kitchen to meet us when Alice and I get back from our walk. He wordlessly pours three glasses of water. I watch him as he cuts a lime into precise wedges and adds one to each glass before handing one to Alice and another to me.

I sip my water, looking out into the sunlit garden. Tomatoes are setting on nicely. Basil towers behind flat-leaf parsley, oregano, thyme and chives. A rosemary tree holds court in the opposite bed, nasturtiums rioting over the stone edging that surrounds it. Further down the path are more countrystyle beds, roses climbing trellises and trailing over fences. Standard roses in pots watch, stiff and upright, over low landscape roses with blooms like miniature sunsets in corals, pinks and reds.

The roses are in David's tender care, but the herbs and vegetables are Alice's babies. I wonder if Glenn will live to taste the tomatoes, or if he appreciates the finely chopped fresh thyme and basil that liven the scrambled eggs that are one of the few dishes he can still stomach.

Maybe I'm taking this "truth versus story" thing too far. Some truths don't change, no matter how you look at them. Glenn is dying, his good days are rare and treasured, and we all know the cancer is winning.

It's taking a toll on Alice too. Some days the blue tinge under her eyes says she barely closed them at all the night before. I remember what it was like to doze, eyelids and heart both worn out and heavy, waiting for the slightest sound that says you're needed.

Although it was many doctor's visits later before I had a word for the hot stabbing pain that became part of my daily experience, the fibromyalgia symptoms had started during those days and nights of sleeping on a pallet on a cold concrete floor, watching my father die. I wonder how much of my life I've allowed to be defined by pain.

Emotional pain, physical pain. Beatings, rejection. I brush my fingers over the tip of a half-opened rose in the vase on the counter, remembering David's lesson in perspective. Had I only been able to see the thorns?

David waits until Alice has nearly finished her glass of water, then speaks. "You girls look a bit warm. Alice, do you want to take a shower and maybe lie down for a bit? I'm sure Dixie and I can keep Glenn happy for another hour or so."

Habit driven, her head starts to shake a refusal. She stops. "If you really don't mind . . ." Her voice trails away, but I can see from the hungry look on her face that there is nothing she would like more than the luxury of an unhurried shower and a pillow under her head.

I put my arm around her thin shoulders, feel the sweat at the base of her neck. I give her a quick squeeze and she leans her head toward my shoulder. "Go on," I urge her. "I'll keep Glenn company for a while, and we can come and get you before he needs his meds."

"Okay, Dixie Rose, I will." Her head stays inclined toward me for another moment before she straightens and heads for the stairway. "I know he's in good hands with you and Doctor David," she adds as she starts up, holding to the banister, moving through a molasses of tiredness that I hope will be eased at least for a while by hot water and cool sheets.

David waits until she is out of sight, then refills our glasses from the pitcher of filtered water from the fridge.

"He's having a really rough day." He means Glenn, of course. His voice is thick, the light tenor has none of its usual amusement. "I can't see that there are any clinical changes, and he says he isn't hurting, but he's pretty blue. I think you'd be good for him, but you needn't sit with him if it will bring you down."

"I don't think blue will rub off on me," I pat his hand and am surprised when he puts his other hand over mine and clings for a moment. Glenn *must* be having a rough day if David is in need of comfort.

"Why don't you get out in the sunshine? Go talk to the roses, they're never blue." It's a joke between us, that the reason no one has been able to breed a blue rose is that roses are too *happy* to be blue.

He smiles. Any other time he would have laughed.

He ruffles my hair on his way to the patio door. No one has ruffled my hair in longer than I can remember.

I've become accustomed to the squeak my running shoes make on the hardwood hall floor. Today it seems abnormally loud, and I stop after a couple of steps to pull them off, padding silently on bare feet the rest of the way to Glenn's room.

The hiss of the oxygen tank is familiar, the big club chair takes me into its embrace, surrounding the contours of my body like a lover of long standing.

Glenn's face is turned toward the window. Sunlight filtering through the silvery blue weave of the drapes gives his face and the creamy bedspread an underwater quality. His eyes are closed, and his breathing doesn't change as I sink into the chair. He doesn't need me here if he is sleeping, but it is comforting to let the chair cradle my body while my mind relaxes into the near silence of the room.

A movement near the door, a flash of red as the slim figure enters the room. Today it's a loose-fitting tank top over black leggings. She perches on the arm of my chair, knees drawn up to meet her chin, arms wrapped tight around them. Her eyes are on Glenn, her face composed as always.

I don't realize I've drifted into a light doze until I feel the chair shift as the girl slides to her feet. Disoriented, I open my eyes to find her standing next to the bed talking to Glenn in a voice too soft for me to make out the words.

She pats his shoulder and, turning to me, leans over for a brief hug before leaving the room. I look back to Glenn, meet his forget-me-not blue eyes. No need to dissimulate with him, he won't appreciate it. "I hear you're having a rough day, can I make it better?"

He smiles a little at my directness, appreciating my saving him the discomfort of pretending his usual cheer.

"Tell me a story," he begins. "Tell me about your father."

I'm taken back to my first visit to this house, reeling from the dream and fighting to uncover my own truth. About my father, about me, about what we really were to each other. That, I hope, is not what he wants to know about my father.

"He was a powerful man." I stop, that isn't where I would have expected to start my story. "I don't mean he was powerful in society, or had a lot of status. He wasn't a leader, in fact, he was very much a loner. But he didn't like to let anything beat him."

I go on to tell Glenn all I'd learned about my father's power. The stories I'd heard of him as a young man, working the loading docks, taking on challenges from bigger men in the competitions, performing impossible feats of strength. And winning. He was a safe bet if you were a betting man.

He was a force to be reckoned with, through sheer strength and stubbornness.

That same strength could lift a little tow head onto his solid shoulders and carry her for hours if needed. Or hold me up to pick the cherries or persimmons that grew just out of reach of grownup arms.

I remember for Glenn the fun times, setting up tents and cooking over open fires or heating water for sponge baths over the little propane burner. I tell him about my father's fierce love of self-sufficiency, how he never outgrew the "I'll do it myself" pride of a willful two-year-old.

"I think that's originally why he wanted the big garden, to be self-sufficient. But it turned into a game, an adventure. When they moved onto that property, the same year that I was born, the soil was more clay than dirt. Nothing would grow in it and the crawdads left holes big enough to hold a golf ball. So they started adding stuff. Every year, more straw, more sand, more old manure. More tilling, more turning, more shoveling. They composted every bit of organic matter they could. Egg shells and coffee grounds, carrot and potato peelings, cut grass and rotten straw. It all went into the compost bin. Which had to be turned, and watered.

"But," I smile at the picture, "we had the most beautiful garden in all creation. We could have fed an army out of that garden every year. We *worked* like an army, that's for sure. It had to be weeded and hoed, picked and cleaned, canned or frozen. We still had plenty to share, even though we put up enough to have vegetables on the table all year long.

"I think my father saw it as a competition with the soil. It wanted to be clay and useless. He said, 'You *will* feed me.' And it did. That's power."

I pause unintentionally. Most things did what my father decided they would do. I'm wondering if I was the only thing in his life that continually refused to bend to his will, but I don't want to wonder that aloud.

"So, let me guess, you didn't always do what he said you *would* do?" Glenn has had too many years observing the spaces where people interact, not to guess the effect my father's power would have had on me. Or maybe the effect my reaction to his power would have had on him. I have a little of that talent of hearing between the lines; Glenn is a master.

"Oh, I was a trial," I try to laugh it off. "I'm sure he despaired of me many times over. But he finally agreed I came out okay after all."

"I'm sure he did. You came out a bit *better* than okay, in spite of his despair. Or was it *because* of it?"

My eyes snap to meet his. His face is impassive, eyes resting calmly on my face. But I sense a tension in the line of his jaw, an effort to his casual tone of voice.

"How well do you think you knew him? You were what, twenty-one, when he died?"

"I was twenty-three." I stop, the unexpected lump in my throat has to shift before I can speak again. "How well did I know him? Glenn, I don't think I got to see the real person behind his face until he accepted that he was dying. Then in that last year I learned to know him like I've never known another person. And I miss him like I've never missed anyone in my life."

I watch his eyes close and his face soften. I look away. I hear his breathing shift, and when I look back at his face, I see that he is sleeping. His hands, clenched around the top edge of the spread before, are lying limp. The tension in his jaw has loosed, the crease between his brows has flattened. If it weren't for the slight rise of his ribs I would not be sure his spirit still occupied the wasted form there on the bed.

I sit in the stillness of his sleep, replaying the stories I've shared. It comes to me, finally, what I'd shown him. Not the thorn, but the rose.

I've come to look forward to my "go-back nights," even though some of the trips have been to dark places I'd tried to forget. Better to revisit them in the semi-safety of sleep with my warrior-sister-spirit as a guide. Whether she is "real" or not, it makes the experiences easier somehow. I am also finding balance by remembering many joyful scenes that I have left untouched for years, learning to see both the thorns and the blossoms.

As though my recounting for Glenn my father's battle with the soil brought me back to the summers of my childhood, the next several nights are jumbles of homey scenes; snapping green beans, or shucking corn in the shade of the old pear tree, kneeling in the strawberry patch eating one for every three or four I pick.

I dream the evenings as well, learning to play ping pong with my father – the old kitchen table stretched to its fullest length and the net fastened securely in the middle. He never let me win, but he patiently showed me how to break my wrist just as the paddle hit the ball to send it back over the net lightning fast and unreturnable. He cheered as hard when I won as when I didn't.

One night, I dreamed of making his favorite Sunday supper – bowls of fresh popped corn and homemade chocolate pudding still warm from the pan. Dreaming his laughter, I'd winked at the girl in red standing next to the stove, watching me stir the pudding. And woke smiling, wanting pudding and popcorn for breakfast.

There have been a few discomforting dreams too, but I'm learning to tell story from truth.

My little red book has this to say:

We can never remember the truth of an experience, no matter how precisely we remember the events. Because every experience we've had since then, even the taking in of a breath, the passing by of a thought, creates a filter through which we see the pictures of the past.

And on the opposite page;

Truth isn't held in facts or in happenings, nor yet in the physical manifestation of people and things, but in the marks they leave behind. The mark it makes on you to read this, and on me to write it – that mark is real and true, and will never pass away.

That's what I'm beginning to understand: that it isn't that any of these events were gifts, but that they all forced me to choose, and coming back over and over to the truth of those choices – that has been, and continues to be, the gift.

I fall asleep each night thinking of the mark these truths are leaving, on me, and on whom else? As the next page of the little red book reminds me:

The stone, once it has pierced the surface of the pool, goes on following its course, unaware of how far reaching are the ripples left in its wake.

Certainly I can see the ripples of my dreams as they touch my immediate circle. I see them in my mirror, a face that is softer, younger, eyes unshadowed by pain or sleepless nights. I know Tom has benefited from those ripples, and so have my clients.

Glenn and Alice have felt those ripples, and even David, although David seems so perfectly self-contained it's hard to imagine how my ripples might leave a mark on him. Vincent, too, has been touched by the ripples; I hope someday he'll let himself take it in. Right now he is still awkward with me, staying far away from the mark our conversation about abuse has left on his world-view.

But even that mark, I'm sure, will prove to be for the good. I hope that the ripples find their way to Vincent's heart and stir a little compassion there, not only for those he perceives as abused, but also for those he believes are to blame. Perhaps those are the ripples I will never see.

But the ripples I *can* see are enough. I look forward to the nights when I dream, and remember, and wake feeling lighter and wiser and more alive than I have felt in all my life.

Friday night. I take a long shower, letting myself relax under the spray. Slip into a silky chemise and under the covers. Only a sheet and a light spread. It's early July; summer is at the height of her reign.

I close my eyes, wait for the movie to start.

Immediately I know I don't want to go here. I can *hear* my voice, or is it only my mind voice, "No, no, no, no!" But the theater is dark, the doors are barred, the dreamer is not permitted to wake.

Her hair is sunbleached to ruddy gold, parted front to back and pulled into two long braids. I can see the white line the part makes down the back of her head as she lies face down on the bed. A flashlight propped on the pillow in front of her provides barely enough light to see the book just inches from her nose. It's summer then too, the fan in the window might have made the room bearable, but it isn't turning. Covers thrown off, thin cotton gown, sturdy brown legs, feet waving in the air as she avidly devours the story. Just turned eight years old a week ago.

We both hear the footsteps. I hiss, "Run, hide, scream!" but she has her own panicked monologue going on.

I know what she's thinking. I know she is wrong.

"Please don't let him see the light, please don't let him catch me reading, please don't, please don't." That isn't what she should be praying for.

I know. But she isn't listening to me.

She snatches the flashlight, clumsily flipping it off before shoving it between the mattress and the wall. The book goes under the pillow, her arms wrap around it protectively. She lies motionless, heart pounding, holding her breath.

If she holds still, there in the newly darkened room, if she doesn't twitch a muscle, doesn't even breathe, she will be safe. He will see that she is sleeping, just as she is supposed to be, and he will go away.

That's what she thinks.

I know better.

The door opens.

He comes in quietly. He sits on the bed.

She doesn't move. She's stopped thinking. She is focused on being still. Sleeping still, death still, not-here still.

I try to dream her into motion. "Wake, live, run, be not-here *moving!*"

She is still.

He lays one hand on her shoulder, it twitches slightly under the thin cotton and suddenly me-now is one with me-then. I *feel* his hand. The dreamer is gone, and I am only here-now in a then I've tried to pretend never happened.

I'm waiting for his voice. For the accusation. "Reading a story book again weren't you? When you were *told* to go to bed!"

Juggling the odds. Better to admit it, yield up the book and the flashlight and take the punishment? Or deny that I had not been able to put my book down and sleep? He wouldn't believe me. Which would be more satisfying for him? To catch me in a lie or to force me to admit my guilt? How should I answer? *When* is he going to ask the question?

Maybe he won't even ask this time. Maybe he'll just assume.

I'm waiting for the first blow. Anticipating.

Sooner-started-sooner-ended. Come-on-just-get-it-over-with. Punish-me-and-we'll-all-go-to-sleep. Stop-playing-around-and-hit-me. I dare ya!

My thoughts are escalating now, needing to know what's next, needing the familiar pattern of accusation, denial, punishment, safety. Might as well comeonjustgetitoverwithNOW!

My eyes are squeezed shut, my head in my arms, the end of one braid tickling my chin. I feel his hand stroking my shoulder, almost a caress.

I'm confused. I can't take the suspense. I move my head off my arms, start to push myself upright.

Immediately he has both my wrists in his hand. His other hand is still on my shoulder. But now it's not caressing. Now he is pushing, trapping, holding me painfully hard against the mattress, stretching my arms full length over my head, closed fists sliding through the gap between the mattress and the headboard, brushing the plaster wall, my head turned on the pillow barely enough for me to breathe, the book hard as a stone under my cheek.

We've never danced this dance of me helpless, him silent. He's never started the punishment without the accusation. I need to know the rules, understand the penalties, what is it he wants from me?

He's standing now. Leaning over me, nearly all his weight pressed against my shoulder, other hand pulling my arms straight until I feel the strain in my arm sockets. I try to squirm away, try to twist to see him.

The accusation, when it comes, is nothing I can understand.

"You like that? Do you? You're a little tease aren't you? Look at you squirm."

If I *could* answer I don't know what I'd say. I can't get my head off the pillow enough to breathe let alone speak, but it doesn't matter, I am without words.

The voice goes on. Alternately pleading and accusing. "You like that don't you, don't you, don't you?"

His weight is off my shoulder. Now I am paralyzed by fear, not pain. I'm afraid to struggle, I don't want to be a "tease." I don't know what is next, but he hasn't hit me yet.

His grip on my wrists has loosened a little but as soon as I move my hands it tightens again. His other hand is moving down my back, brushing my lower back and the curve of my buttocks. I cringe, that is so often where the blows fall. But his touch is gentle. "Tease?" Maybe he is teasing me. Is that the new game? Wait for me to relax, *then* the pain comes?

"Don't pretend," he's whispering again. "You think you're scared, but you want it, you know you do."

"Want WHAT?" A silent scream. "Want you to touch me? Yes, but not like this. Want you to hit me? No, but at least then I'd know what to do. Want you to stop?"

I can't answer that. There is a part of me that wants to believe that this gentle touch is exactly what it seems to be, a sign of love, an offer of comfort, a caress.

But my trapped wrists won't let me accept that. He is saying "You want it, you want it, you want it," over and over and I do but I don't, and I don't know what "it" is.

I can't answer. The pillow stops me. My fear stops me. My confusion stops me. My want stops me. And then, there's the pillow.

I want him to let me turn over so he can hug me. I think he used to do that, when I was a baby. That would be okay to want.

I want him to let go of my wrists so that I can take my face out of the pillow to breathe. That would be okay to want.

It would even be okay to want him to go away. I wouldn't understand, but I could pretend it didn't happen. I *do* want that.

What I want most is for him to talk to me. I want him to tell me what *he* wants. Tell me about that thing he says I want. I know it isn't a good thing. He is disgusted with me for wanting it. But I don't know what it is.

An impasse. With one hand he holds my wrists while I hold my breath. With the other he strokes my back and I relax.

Then his hand is sliding under my gown. His other hand grips my wrists so hard I feel the bones rubbing together, he's leaning above me so close I can feel him breathing, his fingers are tugging at my panties.

Now I am sure. This is *not* what I want. I can feel *his* terror, feel *his* knowing, this is not what *he* wants either.

He doesn't seem to know it isn't what he wants. He lets go of my wrists so he can pull my panties all the way off. I know I should use my new freedom to fight. Instead I wrap my arms around my pillow. I barely notice the thud as the book falls from its hiding place to the floor.

I hear the sound of a belt buckle. Almost, I'm relieved. He is going to whip me after all. But I hear no sound of the belt coming free of the loops.

The sound of a zipper. And his hands are on me again. Pushing my thighs apart. I hug the pillow tighter, not knowing but dreading.

He lifts my hips, pulls my body back toward him. My cotton gown bunches up around my waist. I clutch the pillow, bringing it with me as I slide across the sheets. I hold still, wait, for what is next.

He's stretched out above me. I can feel his body, hotter even than the room. There is something hard pressing between my legs. Only a moment of bewilderment before pain blossoms, numbing my whole midsection. The hard thing is *inside* me, he's never hurt me *inside* me before. Blood drains from my face, my feet are ice, every bit of energy and warmth rushes to comfort the place where I have been stabbed.

I muffle a scream against the pillow. Pain becomes rhythmic as his body stabs me again and retreats. With every stab I press my face harder into the pillow. With every retreat I pretend he is going to stop.

Dots are swimming on the inside of my eyelids. I try to focus on them, to be not-here. I pretend I'm floating there, with those dots, not attached to my body. I'm swimming in stars, not associated in any way with the little girl body being invaded there on that bed. Not even aware of the girl and the man and the rhythm that almost-barely makes the bed frame creak.

I come back from swimming with the dots behind my eyes, and realize he has stopped. He pulls away. It hurts almost as much when he takes it out as when he put it in.

The sound of the zipper again, and the belt buckle. Reverse terror.

Awkwardly he puts my panties back on me. It's difficult for him because I don't move. I've gone baby-angel-on-a-monument stiff, every part of me heavy and unyielding. He pulls the sheet over me and whispers one last admonition.

"You asked for it. You don't want to tell anyone you asked for it."

It isn't until after he is gone, and I lay my check on a wet pillow that I realize I cried.

I submitted. Perhaps, for the first time ever.

I cry some more.

When I wake the next morning, I am me-now again, but my pillow is wet.

I don't know how I could have slept – just drifted off into a deep sleep – after that. But sleep I did. I must not have moved all night. I'm stiff all over. The old fibromyalgia, a pain that I haven't noticed in the last month at all, has its claws in me again, I feel it even before I move.

Not only did I sleep, I slept late. The sun is already bright in the west-facing windows. Tom is gone, but both cats are snuggled close, Suki at my feet and Taffy draped over my shoulder, one paw resting at the base of my throat.

My eyelashes are matted, my eyelids tight and swollen. I move the arm not weighted by a blonde furball and rub my eyes. The resulting sharp-hot-paralyzing pain that stabs at my shoulder blades, elbows, and wrists brings me fully awake.

The cats aren't happy when I finally move again. Taffy tries to stop me by extending her claws ever so slightly. She knows better than to get serious with those needle points, she's just making a statement that she would really, really rather I stayed put. When it's clear that I am determined to sit up, she rises and stretches full length, yawning, as if to say "Well, I was just leaving any way." Taffy is a perfect illustration of why female cats are called "queens."

Suki is less gracious. He wails a protest as I roll him off my feet so that I can move them to the floor. Part Siamese, part who-knows-what, the little tom cat has something to say about almost anything, and he says it at a volume that is startling from such a small animal.

The pain jabbing at my body makes me want to wail along with him. I've missed yoga and my walk with Vincent; he would have given up on me an hour ago.

I doubt he worried. We've continued to walk together but, since that last conversation, he hasn't suggested hanging out over coffee. There is an uneasy distance between us, things not said, things not sayable.

Feeling at least ninety-five, I inch my way to the bathroom, holding onto furniture along the way, and turn the taps to "hot."

Showered, the pain reduced to tolerable, I curl into a big club chair. I have a cup of hot tea and a blanket in spite of the heat already seeping through the patio slider and big bay window. Both cats have followed me here, Suki still vocalizing his displeasure at the relocation of his human cuddle-mate, Taffy strolling in and levitating to the back of my chair as though this was, after all, where she thought we should have been to begin with.

I close my eyes, and the images and tears form in unison. Last night's "go-back" scene plays, faithful to every detail, in an endless loop. "Where were you?" I demand from my warrior child, secret sister, spirit guide. "Why weren't you there with me?"

Then I remember the second dream. The aftermath. The dream that bridged from being one with me-then back to being observing me-now. Still trapped in the dreamscape, watching the two children on the bed.

There I am, the child crying into an already soaked pillow. The adult me gasps at the spot of blood on the sheets. I remember hiding it under the bedspread the next day and sneaking the sheets into the washer as soon as my parents were both out in the garden working. Remember setting the washer to "cold" because that's what my mother did every time I got hurt and got blood on my clothes. Remember taking them out of the washer and looking to see if the spot was washed clean, and the sob of relief when not a trace showed on the sheets.

Watching, the dreaming me remembers, and remembers that this won't be the last time. It won't happen often, but will happen again. And again. And again. The same footsteps. The same held breath. The same me, pinned, helpless, dreading the caress, the hissed words, "you want it, you know you do." The same hot tears.

In my dream, the girl in the red cotton dress sits motionless. Her face, usually so serene, is tight, angry. Her hands, usually laid loosely on her knees, are in fists in her lap.

"Why, Dixie?" it comes out in a hiss. "Why did you just *let* him?"

The child me sits up, reaches for the covers. It's hot in the room, but I understand her need to be covered, to be cocooned in something soft, even a light bedspread.

With the coverlet bunched under her chin, her braids trailing down each side of her face, and eyes red and swollen from crying, she looks like any child after a bad dream. This time I know there is no comfort that I, or anyone, can offer. This is a nightmare that isn't going to end even when he doesn't come again.

"What *should* I do?" the child whispers. "I cried. He didn't stop. She said if I cried he would stop."

How many times had my mother said, "If you would just cry he'd stop." I'd never cried, never let him know he'd won, before. This time I cried. But he did not stop.

"But you didn't even fight! You just laid there and cried. You *always* fight! You *never* cry! You closed your eyes! You *never* close your eyes! You wouldn't even look at *me*, you wouldn't listen to me, I couldn't touch you. YOU SHUT ME OUT!"

The dreamer is astonished. My spirit sister, always calm and composed, is ready to do battle. And she is angry, not with *him*, but with me! What had I said that day we found each other again in a patch of clover? "She has my stubbornness, and certainly my compassion, but the passion has missed her completely." I was wrong.

In my dream, the child that was me is suddenly motionless. As though they have changed roles, *her* face becomes serene and still. She pushes back a wisp of hair escaped from its braid. She wipes her eyes with the back of her hand, rubs at her nose. Takes a deep breath that shudders only a little as she releases it.

"He didn't mean to hurt me." She says it quietly, suddenly sure.

"He only wanted to love me. He doesn't know how."

Sitting in the chair, overheating with the sun and the tea and the blankets and the furry little furnaces that are snuggled close, I remember her voice from my dream, feel again her calm surety, truth ringing in her little girl whisper.

"He just wants me to let him love me. He wants *me* to love him. And I do."

I'm dozing in my chair when Tom comes up from the basement.

"Hey, sweetie." His voice pulls me into now-time. I'm sweat-drenched under my blanket. Even Suki must have gotten too warm; he's curled in his basket in the shade of the chair opposite me.

I stretch, arms overhead, kicking free of the blanket. Taffy lets out a little "merrrrt" to let me know she's still on the back of my chair and doesn't appreciate arms stretching just over her sleeping body.

I laugh. She's so delightfully predictable. The world-as-we-know-it could end, and that cat would only resent the interruption of her nap.

"Yeah, babe?" I stand up, marveling that except for the natural stiffness of sleeping in an unnatural position, my body doesn't protest. I stretch again just to be sure. Not a pang from shoulders, knees, or hips.

"I was thinking about lunch, wanna go somewhere? Mia Rosa sounds good."

It sounds good to me too. A little family-owned Mexican spot, it's a favorite as much for the friendly service and good natured ribbing of the staff as for the food. Sounds like just the touch of familiar I want right now.

"Sure. Let me take a shower and throw some clothes on, okay?"

My second shower of the day rinses me free of the last remnants of both of the dreams. I shampoo my hair, it feels so good to be able to scrub at my scalp without screams from my shoulders. Rubbing conditioner through the strands, I feel the roughness of split ends. I'm past due for a haircut. Maybe

I'll even spring for color.

Hair wrapped in a towel, I scrutinize my face in the bathroom mirror, searching for the child's features in the reflection. Eyes. I find her first in the eyes. Sea-change green and blue, the iris ringed with a navy band. Mood shifts have always shown up first in my eyes. Emerald under the influence of strong emotion. Aquamarine when I'm at ease. Right now they're a hazy green.

My nose is slightly thinner, a necessary change when the surgeon removed the splinter of bone left from the broken bone I didn't know I had. But it still wrinkles when I laugh, even though I laugh less than the younger me once did. My mouth is still her rosy pout, and if I smile less often than the child, at least I smile more often than the adult I'd been just last year.

"If the child felt so unloved, so abused," I challenge my mirror image, "why did she laugh and smile so much? Answer me that!"

My reflection gives no response.

AUGUST

I climb the worn stone steps carefully, resting my hand against the curve of the stone wall for balance. The outside wall of the little castle is hot in the mid-afternoon sun, but in the circular stairwell, the cool damp of morning still prevails.

I'd seen her waving to me from the parapet wall as soon as I got out of the rental car, the familiar blaze of her red dress unmistakable. I emerge on the roof to join her and find her perched on the edge of the wall, looking out over fields and prairie, with her feet dangling over the outside edge. Instinctively, I open my mouth to tell her to get down, at least turn around so that her feet are on the *inside,* for heaven's sake!

Then I remember what she is. If I protest aloud she'll probably jump, just to remind me of what I already know – she may *appear* to be flesh and blood, but she isn't bound to the same limitations as the rest of us "mere mortals."

I lean against the wall beside her. "So how old are you, really?" I blurt it out, then wish I could pull it back, just flick it off the tip of my tongue and down my throat like a frog pulls in a fly. If I know she only *appears* to be flesh and blood, why would I think she would have a chronological age?

"What makes you think I'm an age?" She echoes my thought. "How can a spirit be an age? Only our physical shells are an age. We, our *real* selves, are forever without the need of calendar or clock. Which," she adds, "you know as well as anyone."

"Well, okay." Silence except for the thud of her heels as she swings them against the stone wall.

Feeling suddenly brave, I hoist myself to the wall next to her. I keep my feet on the *inside,* and my hands rooted firmly to the wall on either side of me, but the thought of all that nothing at my back doesn't scare me. Much.

"So what should I call you? Do you have a name?"

"You *could* call me 'Dix,' that way we wouldn't get us mixed up." She's teasing me, I can tell.

"So your name is Dixie too?"

"No, I'm not Dixie Two." Now she's laughing outright. "But of course, we bear the same name. How could it be otherwise since we are one?"

"What does that mean?"

I'm asking what she means that we are one, but she chooses to answer a different question.

"Lionheart. Just like 'Richard.'" Her voice goes lecture-on-demand formal. "The name 'Dixie' is the feminine diminutive of 'Richard' and has the same meaning. They may not sound a lot alike, but think of the nicknames – 'Dick' and 'Dix,' or even "Dickie' and 'Dixie.' Or some say it is the feminine diminutive of 'Benedict.' Which means 'blessing.' A blessing of bravery, that's us."

I drink that in. It isn't necessarily sweet. More like tonic water, sharp, laden with quinine, but thoroughly refreshing. I don't even laugh at the incongruity of the phrase "feminine diminutive" coming from what *looks* like a little girl.

"You chose the name we needed to have," she says gently, laying one small, slim hand over mine where it clenches the top of the wall. "You named us to be brave in our hearts and a blessing to all we meet."

We sit in companionable silence for a time. I forget to be afraid of the nothing at my back.

"I miss him," I say, barely a whisper. I know she can follow the trail of thought.

Family story says my mother had decided on 'David' if I were born a boy. But my father and my sister were locked in a battle over girl's names. My sixteen-year-old sister was of a romantic mind and wanted something eloquent and flowery; my father was a pragmatic type who wanted something sweet and simple. After "Veronica" and similar names were vetoed by my father as being too fancy, and "Mary" and other names of four letters were dismissed by my sister as being too plain, my sister saw a newspaper article about a woman named "Dixie Diane."

She declared that was the perfect name should the unexpected child turn out to be a girl. My father, who had known a "Dixie" and apparently thought well of her, agreed. So when I think of choosing my name, I think of my father.

And I do. I miss him. I wonder if he guessed at the significance of the name they chose for me; how I would need the brave heart, how the blessing would touch us both.

"Miss him? How can you miss him? Do you think he's really gone?"

"Well, he's not *here*." I spread my arms and waver for a moment. I tuck my heels hard against the stone to steady myself, but manage to avoid grabbing for the wall.

"I understand he isn't really dead, his spirit isn't anyway. But he isn't available to me anymore.

"And I miss him."

I repeat it stubbornly, dropping my hands back to my knees and leaning forward just a smidgeon. Not enough to betray that moment of panic as my arms went wide and my shoulders tilted back, but enough to feel a little safer on my perch.

"Ah. He isn't?

"But you *do* understand that life is eternal. Love is eternal. It's only the physical body, the *illusion* you project when confining yourselves to limitations of time or space, *that* body cannot last forever. You do understand *that*, yes?"

"Of course. I understand that. But I still miss being able to see him, talk with him. I miss his presence in my life."

"Ah."

"Ah," I have learned, is her equivalent of David's "Mmm." It means, "Challenge your premise, because I'm not going to do it for you." It means, "No comment, because any comment I make would be something you aren't ready to hear."

"Have you ever asked yourself why? Why your father did what he did?"

"Of course." The direction she's chosen surprises me, but it's a question I can answer.

"I've asked that a lot. I think he was afraid of losing control. I was his daughter, his possession. He *should* be able to control me. It challenged his manhood that he couldn't manage even a little girl.

"And I was his responsibility. How I looked, how I behaved, reflected on him. If he lost control of me it would show he couldn't do his job, what would people think?

"And I was his burden too. A late-in-life baby he didn't plan for, and probably didn't want."

"So why did he rape you? Was that to control you too?"

"No."

I let that word sink into the air and the stone around us. Feel it on my tongue like salt melting, getting slowly more and more bitter.

"No. That wasn't about control. I'm sure a lot of well-trained professionals would tell me I'm in denial. But I was there, they weren't. Never mind the facts, or the events, or what all their studies say it means. My spirit knows the truth.

"He *needed* to control me, but what he *wanted* was intimacy.

"For *me*, intimacy is communicated on so many levels. Words, a hug, the meeting of eyes, a wink, a secret smile." I squeeze her hand to illustrate. "To *me* these are all physical signs of intimacy of spirit." He couldn't understand that; he was embarrassed by how intimate I could be with people, even as a child.

"But I think he envied it too. And he craved it. So he tried to take it from me. Sex was the only kind of intimacy he understood."

Without warning, I'm overwhelmed with sorrow, understanding his desire, understanding the emptiness he felt, not being able to fill that need.

I hear the double meaning in my words, "tried to take it from me." Yes, both. He tried to take it *away* from me, tried to break the free and generous spirit that connected easily with other spirits. And tried to take the intimacy he wanted from me. By force.

"Intimacy," I turn to meet her eyes, shifting my weight cautiously on the narrow wall. "Intimacy has to be *invited*. It has to be *granted*. He could *not* take it from me that way. It is a dance of permission. Without the invitation and permission, intimacy cannot be created, no matter the physical activity."

I'm not talking to her. I hope the soul I'm talking to can hear.

"When that dance *is* danced," I finish softly, "when it is danced by two souls who ask and agree, invite and accept - then it can be expressed with or without words, with or without touch, with or without a physical body."

"Ah." She says again. This time it is the acknowledgment of a bright light dawning.

I hear the echo of my words, "with or without a physical body." The echo sounds so sure, but I have my doubts.

"So what are *you* really? I know that physical body *you're* wearing is just a convenience. Something you decided to manifest to make it easier for *us* to be intimate. That isn't what you are.

"So what are you? My twin soul? My spirit guide? My older, wiser self?"

Her laughter stings a little. I'm missing the obvious.

"What do you *want* me to be?" She spreads her arms wide, and I clench my fists to keep from snatching at her dress. Remind myself she is not going to go tumbling off the wall.

"I always wanted a twin," I admit. "My mother said she kind of hoped I'd be twins because she didn't want to raise an only child, and with the other two kids grown and gone, that's what I was. She soon decided one of me was plenty."

We share a wink. I feel my nose crinkle as I smile, and notice hers does the same.

"I guess what I have is a twin who never lived." I correct my language quickly. "I mean a twin who didn't manifest on this plane as a human infant the way I did."

"Closer. I just never agreed to the perceived limitations of 'human' the way you did. You are no more limited than I am, you just choose to confine yourself to what you expect of a 'human' existence.

"You're having experiences I can't have, not having chosen to limit my *self* in that way, just like I'm having experiences you can't have unless you surrender those beliefs of limitations.

"Sometimes, though, a choice that looks unwise from my perspective is exactly the choice you need to make in order to become the person you chose to be. *You* taught me that."

"I taught you? I taught *you* about choices?"

"Yes, Little One," we smile at the shared secret of her pet name for the child I had been, "*you* taught *me*.

"I didn't anticipate your father's coming to your room, and what he did there. I didn't understand how you could choose to submit to such a thing. You told me why. And you were right. You didn't *have* to submit, but it taught him something he could not have discovered any other way. And it taught me something too."

"What? What did it teach you?"

"That truth," she pauses. Deliberates. I can almost see her selecting and discarding words.

"Truth isn't an absolute. Truth can be chosen in the same way you select any other possibility, for the same *reasons* you choose any other possibility.

"We choose our *possibilities* for where they will take us, what they will help us become. You showed me we can choose our truths the same way. You said it to your friend, Vincent, 'We choose who we become by choosing our life.'

"But you chose who you are, not only by choosing the *events* of your life, but choosing what they meant to you. You chose your life by choosing your truth."

I shake my head. "I don't understand."

"I saw only abuse and control. *You* saw an attempt at intimacy.

"When he told you not to tell, I heard a threat. *You* heard the plea.

"What he did, I called it rape. *You* called it love.

"The truth *you* chose, it's been your path to who you have become. If you had believed *my* truth, you would have become like me. A warrior who'd forgotten that the battle is only a game. A child who'd forgotten that the gift of childhood is to *play*. You'd have been stone inside. The same stone *I* was until you called me back and showed me your truth: that it was rape, and just as horrid and wrong as I thought it was, but it came from a place of love, a desire for oneness, and while that didn't change the wrongness of the act, neither did the act obliterate the love. The rose and the thorn are both true, but my truth saw only the thorn."

I want to tell her that for a long time I did believe her truth because it was the truth that was reflected all around me. In the books I read, the movies I saw. I heard it from professionals with initials after their names to prove that they knew more about my mind than I did. I heard it in my imagination every time I considered telling a friend, "I am not the person you think that I am; here is what you do not know about me."

"You gave *him* the mercy of that truth as well." Her voice cuts across my unspoken thoughts. "You showed him that that was not love, but you showed him too, what love really is. You didn't make him admit that what he did was wrong, you gave him the space to make it *right*.

"You offered him the option of a truth that was *his* path to the person he wanted to be. A father who loved his daughter. Just that simple. And who was loved, in turn. The simplest truth we ever uncover. Love."

At length we both move, in unchoreographed unison, me hopping down from my perch almost as easily as she from hers. She comes to me and puts her arms around my waist, leans her head against my shoulder. I wrap my arms around her and stroke her hair, so like my own before the streaks of white appeared.

I open the bag I'd carried with me up the stairs, pull out a blanket and the selection of cheeses, crackers and chocolates I'd picked up at the grocery before driving out. Fresh fruit and bottles of water follow. She spreads the blanket over the sun heated concrete roof top and we settle in.

"I missed a lot," she says, apple in one hand and cracker in the other. "After you sent me away. I could watch you, but I couldn't hear your thoughts. I could see the results of the choices you made, but I couldn't understand what led you to those choices.

"I heard what you told David. I didn't want you to see me, but I was there. You said you decided to die because you believed your life didn't mean anything to anyone. Why? When you had found a truth so powerful that it got you through the rape and the beatings that were before that, what truth made you believe your life was worthless?"

I stop chewing. A need to swallow forces me to move my jaws, teeth coming together without conscious thought to reduce the bite of pear into something that will go down my throat.

I remember the night I realized he wasn't coming back to my room. The night the dread of hearing his steps turned to fear that I would never hear them again. A spring day, the school year nearly finished. Me, on the verge of fourteen. Frozen on the threshold of the world. Teetering on the brink of selfdom. Huddling under the covers in a suddenly chilled room in the Kansas heat of late May. "He doesn't want me to love him anymore."

How long have I avoided remembering that night? Longer than I avoided remembering the first night he came to my room. Longer than I avoided remembering the first time he beat me, dancing away from the lash of the pear tree switch. Longer than I avoided remembering screaming in pain and anger listening to the bits of plaster breaking free in the wall as my head connected with it time after time. Longer than any memory I have ever dodged, stuffed, rejected, refused to acknowledge – this one. I had no truth for this one.

"I believed him." I fumble with a slice of cheese, placing it on a cracker, taking it off again. Just to have something to focus on that isn't her watchful face. What to tell her? How to tell her? When I've never thought it through for myself.

My mind scrambles for an answer, finds only stories.

Always I had been a student of story. The story books my father abhorred were my sweetest treats. I hid them behind my text books in class, and devoured them like forbidden bonbons. What homework I had could easily be done at home under his watchful eye where I could never get away with reading what I chose. I read on the school bus and while I ate lunch in the cafeteria. My mind was full of friends who never lived and would never die.

The grade school library offered little to challenge me, and books from the public library were subject to my mother's careful scrutiny. But once I had the Junior High library at my disposal, I began to make my own choices. My reading comprehension was far ahead of my social understanding; as I graduated to classic literature originally intended for adult consumption, I was plunged into a world where being a "good girl" had a whole new set of requirements.

I'd been feeding on a diet of children's stories, worlds where the girls were still girls and many of them tomboys at heart. Now I consumed tales of girls coming into womanhood in an age where beauty, breeding and virginity determined future prospects. I learned that a girl without beauty could be transformed by a good hair dresser and tailor, a girl without breeding could, if she were a beautiful virgin, hope to marry well if she was also sweet, kind, patient and lucky. But a girl without her virginity could hope for nothing.

I'd never accepted the shame my father offered. He believed what he did to me in my room was wrong, I was sure of that. I was bewildered by his insistence that I wanted it, and that my wanting it put the wrong solidly on my shoulders. Certainly I thought, there were better ways to show love than the pain and shame of this, and this would never be my choice, but it seemed to be the only way he knew.

Then came the summer when I took on all the shame of my newly discovered world. That summer I fell in love with a boy I'd only seen once, with the surety that only the innocent can have. That summer I discovered what innocence meant in a young woman and that mine was gone before I knew the price of its loss. That summer I shattered the love that was around me and within me like hail shatters a stained glass window – rent by a loss I couldn't name.

I was damaged goods, forever scarred, my worth as a woman, as a female person, tossed aside.

Punishment took on new color as well. No longer did the words or the blows represent aberrant behavior from a man who loved me and occasionally lost his temper.

Now, with the understanding given to me by "classic literature," he was the villain in the story, just as I was the victim. Immersed in the drama, drowning in a version of my story I had never been privy to before, believing myself worth nothing, I had chosen a truth that I could not live with.

"When he stopped coming to my room," I think I have something I can offer her now, "my truth turned against me. If what he did was his misguided attempt at loving me, and asking me to love him back, then surely if he didn't want to do it anymore, he must not love me.

"Those books make it clear that girls who were raped were victims, their lives ruined unless someone took pity on them. But girls who allowed it, who *wanted* it, they were worse. I didn't want what he did. But I did want his love. And if I wanted him to love me and wanting 'it' made me a bad girl, then I was a bad girl even if I didn't really want it.

"I believed I understood why he punished me, not for anything I *did*, but because I was just bad. And I believed I understood why no one would do anything about it. They knew it too, that I was bad, and I deserved to be punished.

"So it was no surprise when I looked at my face in the mirror and saw those bruises, when I looked at the people who knew me best, and professed to love me dearly, only to have them look away.

"I was only getting what I was 'asking for.' No one could save me from that. And that was the truth I chose.

"That was the worst truth I told myself when I 'fell' to the dirt floor of the hay barn, and when I poured the aspirin into my palm and picked up a glass of water.

"My truth. My choice."

I put the cheese resolutely on top of the cracker and take a bite. I look up, finally meeting her eyes, as she moves a hand to wipe at tear that has escaped to run down her cheek.

She holds the drop of moisture on the tip of her finger and looks from it to me, amazement taking over her features and pausing the flow of tears.

"I'm crying!"

But she isn't, not anymore. She's smiling, gleeful wonder spreading over her face, making her look, for the first time, truly childlike.

"I've never cried!" The tear on her finger is gone, dried by the breeze, but still she holds her finger out between us, testament to her discovery.

I consider telling her that crying is overrated, but I know that isn't true. It is a blessed release, an expression of emotion, a physical manifestation of powerful inner thought. The soul's way of clearing the body from the inside out. Not overrated at all.

"You needn't cry for me, Little One." I savor the pet name on my tongue, it is sweet to comfort her for a change. "It was *my* choice, and I have a lot of gifts to show for it. This," I motion back and forth between us, "this is one of those gifts. I wouldn't change one second of my life if it brought us this."

She takes my hand and holds it between both of hers. "I know. I'm not crying for you. Well, I was, a little bit, but not from sadness. I'm so happy that you took that truth, that ugliness you created in your mind, and you turned it into something so beautiful and rare.

"It's like the roses in winter, isn't it? That David talked about the first time you met. It *looks* like they're suffering, all brown and withered, without leaves or blooms. Nothing that hints at the beauty still inside. But that isn't *their* truth about winter. They've just gone inside of themselves. With the spring they'll come back more beautiful than we remembered. We treasure the beauty, but winter is a necessary phase of it. The rose and the thorn, the beauty and the winter, it's all true.

"You knew the truth about your winters, until you listened to everyone else's stories. Then you believed that winter made you ugly, made you worthless, robbed you of your leaves and blooms and left only the thorns. I'm crying because I am so glad you chose not to make that true."

"I had good gardeners," I say at last.

I squeeze her slender fingers, placing my free hand over hers so that our hands are stacked, one over the other, layers of intimacy and love.

We talk then of little things. I answer her questions of the years that lay between the night I sent her away and the day she rode back into my life, here on this very prairie.

She answers mine of what it is to be free to move as a spirit, without the limitations of needing a human body.

"Why didn't you come back before?" I ask her.

"I never left. I've tried to show myself to you many times, but you were closed. Until that afternoon, out here in the sun and wind. I felt you yearning for home and when I rode by I realized you could see me.

"If I knew then that I could cry, I would have cried with joy."

I smile, remembering my expectation that she and the horse would vanish into the air. Had I believed a little stronger, they might have done just that.

"Why is it so exciting to you that you can cry?"

"I don't know. It makes me feel more real somehow. I chose this body, this *appearance* of a body, when I first came to you. But really, I was just you, another manifestation of your soul self.

"You might think I was 'older and wiser,' but everything that I knew, you knew just as well. I was only there as a way for you to access your own wisdom.

"When you sent me away, I thought I would cease to be. But I didn't. I came to you often, but you couldn't see me, and I couldn't hear you. But even without access to you, I still thought of myself as you, and I was still hard inside with my *own* truth about what he did to us in your room. Even so, I didn't cry."

I understand. I know suddenly why those tears matter. They are *her* tears, manifestation of *her* inner thoughts, *her* emotion. Not a reflection of me; hers and hers alone. That is why other people can see her now, she isn't just me, she is *her* too.

"I think, if you don't mind hearing a little of *my* wisdom, that you are going to need another name. You're welcome to mine, of course you'll always be part of me. But you are your own self too, and that self should have a name."

She laughs, a completely unguarded sound. Uncharacteristic in the child, but so natural coming from this young woman who now shares my meal.

"My own spirit," she echoes me. "*That's* why Alice could see me standing at the door after you and David went inside! I'd become my own self!

"I called myself Rose. When Alice came to the door and asked if she could help me, I was so dumbfounded that she could see me I said the first thing that came to mind. I said my name was Rose, and that I was supposed to be with you.

"She let me in and gave me tea and chocolates. I'd never tasted tea. Or chocolates. Oh, that was lovely!

"We talked about roses, and she took me out into the garden and pointed out her favorites. And she called me 'Little Rose.'

"I liked that too."

Our eyes meet, her nose crinkles with her smile, and I know mine is doing the same.

"Then that is what you shall be, Rose. And only you and I will know you are also me. We're sisters, it will be a good secret for sisters to share."

I reach for the bag, begin packing up the apple cores and cheese wrappers. "Are you riding back into town with me? Or do you have places you want to visit?"

"You are the place I want to visit," she says firmly. "But it is nice to have choices."

The car packed, the steep road down the hill negotiated, we look out across the late summer fields.

"But what if I'm wrong?" I break the silence with a question that has been haunting me. "What if my truth is just wrong?"

Her brow furrows. "How can your truth be wrong?"

"What if I believe something just because I want to? Because it's easier for me." My next words are so quiet a human who couldn't hear my mind voice would have had to strain to hear, "What if I'm just lying to myself?"

She says nothing for a little bit. Finally she asks me a question, "Would it matter?"

I remember asking her about the little mermaid, asking if all stories are just as true as my life. She had answered the same way, "Does it matter?"

"Maybe. If my truth doesn't agree with someone else's, it would matter. Wouldn't it?"

"They will behave in a way that matches their truth, yes. And you will behave in a way that matches yours. It matters, in that it affects the outcome, if your truths are not the same. But that isn't because you are lying to yourself. You cannot lie to yourself about what is true to you."

I see her point; the very truth of it precludes a lie.

"But what about Glenn? It's true that he is dying, isn't it?" I remember standing in the kitchen with Alice and David, wondering if I were taking the "truth versus story" thing a little too far.

"Is he? His body may not be with us much longer, but does that make him dead? Was *I* dead before I had a body? Was my voice only your imagination?

Or was I as real as you? What is your truth?"

"You were part of me. You said so yourself. That's different."

"Is it?"

I drive, lost in thought, not noticing the landmarks, until I realize I've turned into the hotel parking lot, put the car in park, and turned off the engine, all while my mind was on another plane.

I unlatch my seatbelt and turn to face her. "I think I understand. We worked intimacy in reverse, didn't we? We were intimate in spirit, without bodies, first. Most people, we learn intimacy face to face, then, when the body is not present, we find ways to continue the intimacy. It's hard enough if we have to rely on the telephone, or email, or even written letters. It's harder when the other soul no longer has a use for those usual forms of communication. But you're saying we can still share that intimacy of spirit, even when the other person is what we would call dead."

"See," she nods at me. "You do know. I knew you did, because you wrote this." I see that she is holding my journal, finger marking a page. She opens it and begins to read, starting with the title, the poem I had written after that moment of understanding, realizing how much the same my father and I had been.

<u>Intimate Truth</u>

Who knew

That the sea
Keeper of so much restless wisdom
Dreamer of endless mysterious visions
Should yearn, in fact

For the land
Should wait
With bated breath and tide
For the moon to give a signal

Justification and permission
To send a caress of foam
Slipping, sinuous onto the sand

Excuse and opportunity
To take the ragged cliff face
Into a crushing embrace

Invite and passport
To send delirious tendrils
Invading every cranny

Should sigh
When the rhythm of the world
Calls him into himself
Again

Having failed to penetrate as deeply
Enfold as ardently
Or seduce as completely
As he desired

The land
Who longs to come unrooted
To leave her solid moorings
Who cries always for the sea

But that the sea
Would, in fact
Yearn for the next time
His tides carry him to shore

Hmm
Who knew?

"We always want more." She closes the journal. "Whatever we have, we want more. We want longer, we want closer, we want deeper. I think *a lot* of people try to create that through physical intimacy, sexual conquest, but what we really want, is oneness. An invitation home.

"And yet, that invitation is always there. What we yearn for is already ours. We choose the yearning, when the truth is there is *no* power that can pull us apart except our own power. Why is that? It is even true for me, now, and even I do not understand it."

I'm baffled for a moment, trying to connect that poem with my question about death, then I understand.

"We are never separate. We are always one, we are always home. It's like what you said about not agreeing to the limitations of having a human body. But until your body became manifestly real and separate from me, you couldn't know the taste of tea and chocolate.

"I sent you away. You learned to exist as your own self. Illusion of separation, and what a dance we've danced gaining that intimacy again.

"My father saw himself in me, but did not recognize it as himself. Illusion of separation. We danced a dance that could have ended in tragedy, but we found our way to intimacy at last.

"People die. Illusion of separation. What dance do we dance to hold to the intimacy we gained while they were in human form?

"The land and the sea are one, we are one, we accept the illusion of separation because we enjoy the dance.

"Is that the truth? The yearning, the wanting more, wanting closer, deeper, longer, it's just a dance? We could have it all, anytime we're ready to make the choice? Anytime we're ready to end the dance?"

She nods, slowly. "Yes, I think you are right. I, too, have learned to love the dance.

"So we choose our truths, and others must choose their own truths. But when two choose the same truth, they dance the same dance, and they find their way to the oneness that was theirs all along."

We climb the hotel steps in silence. As I unlock the door she says, "Can I have the first shower?"

Finally, a question with an easy answer. "Of course you can, Little Rose."

I sit at the desk, standard hotel issue, thumbing idly through the little red book while I listen to the drumming of water from the bathroom and watch the lingering evening light turn the clouds outside the window into neon shades of rose and blue. Thinking about illusions. And truth.

As my mind wanders through the discoveries of the afternoon, it snags on a barely noticed memory that, like the dying rays of the sun when the clouds move aside, is nearly blinding in its clarity.

I'd become my father's unofficial nurse. Day and night, I was never off duty for long. But everyone insisted that Tom and I deserved a break, so when we heard that Chuck Berry was performing at Worlds of Fun, an amusement park in Kansas City, we agreed to leave Dad in the care of my mother and my aunt and make a day of it. Tom's younger brother and his friend had no clue who Chuck Berry was, but they were thrilled when we suggested a day trip to do the rides and stay for the concert.

I'd fretted throughout the day. Dad had taken to believing that I was the only person who could move him without hurting him, and although I knew that with the cancer eating his bones and the agony of lying in one place day after day there was no escape from pain no matter who was caring for him, I felt guilt at leaving him so long. But as evening came on, boasting a sunset much like the one outside the hotel window right now, and the musicians took the stage, my worry moved aside and allowed the familiar lyrics and guitar licks to blaze their way into my nervous system.

Chuck was in his element. The audience demanded extra encores, and he delivered. By the time we navigated through the emptying park two things were clear: Tom's brother and his friend were newly minted Chuck Berry fans, and we were going to be much later getting home than I had promised we would be.

My dread mounted as we approached my parents' driveway. It was after midnight, and I knew that while we were playing in the late summer sun, it had been another long, anxiety-ridden day for everyone I'd left behind.

As I entered the bedroom, an apology already forming on my lips, my father's eyes instantly locked on mine. Chilled, I said nothing, and he said exactly what I had expected him to say, the words that had been echoing in my skull hour upon hour of the long drive home.

"Where have you been?"

In that moment was encapsulated all the times I'd come home late. The times I'd ridden my bike or one of my horses further than I realized. The times I'd stayed for just one more story, one more song, one more dream, one more game. The times I'd been stuck in tree houses or distracted by a tadpole morphing in the ditch. The times I'd been told to come home, and I didn't come home in time.

But this was not those times. I drew a breath, whether to defend myself or apologize I can no longer say. Because in that drawn breath I heard words he'd never said before. Not to me.

"I'm sorry."

His voice was faint, sounding as though he might have shrunken to something just this side of gone. But his words were clear in the suspended silence that hung between us.

Two words. Carrying entire worlds.

I know that isn't all that was said. I vaguely remember reassuring him, bustling to give him the care he needed. The long overdue repositioning in the bed, smoothing sheets, fluffing pillows, holding the glass and the straw so he could sip some water. Nothing that others hadn't done, but apparently he'd been waiting for me.

I'd escaped finally once my patient had fallen into a light sleep. Tom found me huddled on the back porch step, tears pouring over my cheeks, down my neck, splashing inelegantly off my chin and my nose. I tried to tell him what I'd heard, what it meant, but I'd swallowed my voice with my tears, and no sound came. But he knew. I think he'd heard it too, the words, and all the unsaid meaning behind that quiet apology.

After a while I'd gone to the bathroom to wash the mess I'd made of my makeup, then sat in the chair next to the hospital bed, watching my father's face, my body still feeling the cocktail of rollercoaster thrills, Chuck Berry echoes, and the old dread of punishment and humiliation. Still trying to reconcile what my body was expecting with the quiet voice that had said so simply, "I'm sorry."

I'd been sitting long enough that I'd relaxed a bit. My eyes were closed although I wasn't quite sleeping when I felt him watching me. I lifted my head to meet his eyes, still clear and blue as a lake in winter.

He smiled then, and I found myself smiling back.

I had to lean close to hear his next words.

"Does he still do the duck walk?" he asked, and now those blue eyes were laughing.

"Yeah, Dad," I replied, feeling my smile widen until my nose crinkled.

"Yeah, he still does the duckwalk."

The shower has stopped, I hear Rose humming a light, dancing melody. I notice that the sun has nearly put itself to bed and that I have tears on my cheeks and a smile on my face.

Who knew that my father, enforcer of religious rules that made no room for secular music let alone sinful Rock and Roll, would know anything about the duck walk?

Yeah, who knew?

Time flies by following my Kansas trip. I wake up one Saturday morning to realize it has been two weeks since I've been to a yoga class, since I've walked the park, since I've seen David and his roses, since I've visited Alice and Glen.

I've missed the morning yoga class, but I manage to arrive almost late for the lunchtime power flow class. After my absence from the mat, I'm more than a little afraid the pace and strenuous nature of the power flow class might be too much for me, but I settle into a cross-legged position, wrists on my knees, and begin to take control of my breath. I dismiss my thoughts and let the recorded flute and drum be the only language I allow. On the instructor's cue I roll forward over my crossed ankles, pushing effortlessly back into child's pose without a twinge of pain.

After class I throw my mat in my car and pocket the keys. The early spring day when I'd left class and set out to the park in the cool mist with the fire in my belly seems like a distant yesterday. Today the fire is not only in my belly. It blossoms there, but it also blossoms all around me, sparked by the rays of the Indian Summer sun.

Today I'm thankful for the absence of pain and the easy grace with which I can move through asanas on the mat, but I'm no longer surprised by it. I'm loving the easy way I stride across the street from the yoga studio to the waiting park, but it's not the anomaly it was just a few months ago. Today I don't look for joggers and moseyers on the shaded paths, I look for my friends.

I spot David lounging on a bench, his basket of tools at his feet. His head is back, his eyes are closed. I step off the path into the grass and make my way quietly to the spot behind his bench.

Before my feet have even stopped moving I hear, "Hello Dixie Rose, how was yoga today?"

"There's just no surprising you is there?" I flop down at his feet in amused exasperation. He leans forward with his elbows on his knees and examines my face.

"Oh, you've managed, once or twice, but I'm not going to tell you how."

"Fine," I stick my tongue out in laughing defiance. "Be that way!" I pull my knees up under my chin and wrap my arms around them just because I can. I feel the stretch across my shoulders, the ground firm under my buttocks, but no pain. None.

"What a difference this summer has made." I think for a moment I've spoken my thought aloud, then realize the words had been delivered in David's light tenor.

Perhaps he *can* read my mind. I've heard that he knows a little bit about how that works.

I don't know why I'd been surprised when Alice told me that David had been one of the most sought-after brain surgeons in the Midwest. Picturing my gentle friend slicing brain tissue with the same delicate precision with which he pruned a rose bush or cut a lime into wedges shouldn't have been such a reach.

Maybe it was just the thought of David as a traditional clinician. Or a traditional anything at all. Although from what Alice told me, the traditional path wasn't David's choice even in the hospital setting. Actually, she'd described him as one of the most respected theorists in brain function in the United States and had he been any less brilliant, less respected, or less right, she said they would have eased him out long before he chose to leave.

His theories about brain function had been celebrated and published in medical journals all over the world. But when he put forth his theories about the *mind* and suggested that doctors would better serve their patients by discovering and addressing what was happening there than by running tests, prescribing medications, or even performing surgeries, the medical community had been less than enthusiastic. So, as he'd told Alice and Glen, he'd left the battlefield and the surgical suite behind in favor of roses who listened and nodded and never suggested that he go back to "fixing" sick people.

I don't know if David knew what Alice had revealed, but it had given me a new perspective on the capable way he cared for Glen, the almost magical way he had of catching the nuances of any conversation, and the really irritating way he had of knowing what I was thinking before I'd fully formed the words.

So perhaps his comment is only related to how easily I sink to the ground, or how naturally my knees come to my chin, or how easily my shoulders stretch to allow my arms to wrap around my knees. Perhaps he can see improved right-left brain balance in the way I move. Maybe he's just observing clinical differences I've achieved over this summer. But somehow, I don't think so.

"Yes it has," I agree. "It doesn't feel like the same place it was when we met."

I realize then that the bench he's sitting on now is the same bench he'd collapsed on, laughing as he named himself a climbing rose, nodding at all of us from way high up. Then the roses had just been sharing the winter off their roots. Now they're dropping petals from their summer gowns.

"Is it not the same place," he challenges me, "Or are you not the same person?"

"Yes. Both. Nothing is ever the same, is it? I'm not, you're not, the park isn't." I pause, "Well, you always seem to be the same. But you can't be. Can you?"

He ponders, leaning back on his bench again. He stretches his legs long and his arms wide and tilts his head back toward the afternoon sun.

"No." He brings his gaze back down to where I sit, patiently waiting his response. "I can't be the same. So if I appear to be the same it might suggest I've gotten so set that the changes inside don't show up outside. A rose that stops putting out new growth is bound to get severely pruned. Or die. Thank you for bringing that to my attention."

Now *I'm* surprised. In all our talks I've never ventured to suggest that *he* should change or grow. I wouldn't have even if I'd had an observation to make, but truly he seems so perfectly done growing that I can't think of one thing about him I would change.

I say so and he laughs, a laugh grown so familiar to me I can just *think* of something I want to share with him and I hear him laugh in delighted response even when we're miles apart.

"*Done* growing? You think I'm *done* growing? Oh, Rosy girl, you just wished me into an early grave. We're never done growing. When we stop growing in this lifetime, we move out of it and I'm not finished with this body yet."

I have a protest forming on my tongue, that there is nothing wrong with thinking he's pretty much perfect the way he is, and that I certainly wouldn't wish him into an early grave. I swallow it.

Is that what death is? And end to growing? Is each life just a "growing season" and each death a time to sow anew? I wonder how that ties in with his theories on the brain. And the mind.

"I need to expand my horizons," he goes on. "What would challenge me to change and grow? Do you think I should join a circus? Or maybe I should try deep sea diving. I think right now I'll go play at being doctor again. Alice asked me to sit with Glenn, it seems she has an appointment."

He winks at me as he gets to his feet, mind reading again, I guess. Alice does have an appointment, which is the reason I'm not going with him to sit with Glenn.

I'd made the appointment. I'd promised myself a haircut, then thought of Alice. If a little pampering and change of what I saw in my mirror would be good for my spirits then I was sure Alice needed it even more. So I'd booked for both of us and convinced her that David would be able to keep Glenn comfortable while she and I indulged in a little beautifying and an early dinner.

I watched David cross the park toward the fanciful house on the corner then headed for my car, wondering how he will choose to expand his horizons without joining a circus or heading for the deep blue sea. I'm pretty sure he was just teasing about that.

Late that evening, sitting with my journal and little red book, still thinking about growing, and living, and expanding horizons, I opened to a random page and read.

Horizons are only the limit of our vision, not the limit of our journey.

And on the opposite page,

If you've been looking at the same horizon for too long, it's because you *have not moved.*

Like David, it seems this book reads minds. Or maybe, my mind is written here already.

Alice and I sit over hot tea at her kitchen table. It's a magically spiritual place, the kitchen table. In country cottages that offer no larger room in the house, or in my sprawling suburbia ranch home with the vaulted ceiling over its huge, combined living, dining and kitchen area, the kitchen table is where the hair is let down and the heart is let open.

There are things we can share at the kitchen table that could never be shared in any other space. And things, too, that we can bear.

Even in this city mansion, four stories of solid brick with turrets and balconies jutting off the top floors and a formal foyer, parlor and dining room on the first, we sit most often in the kitchen.

It is a cheerful space, modern while still in keeping with the rest of the house. Wooden cabinet doors painted creamy white stretch all the way to the 10 foot ceiling. A black gas range with six burners, two covered with a flat griddle. Granite counter tops midnight blue flecked with black and gold. But for all the richness apparent in the rest of the furnishings, the kitchen table is just like any table in any old country kitchen, heavy oak, stained and scarred, set now with a plain white tea pot and heavy white mugs.

Alice and I have shared many pots of tea since David first brought me to this house. And stories. So many stories. Our own stories. Stories that touched our lives, some fiction – more important than memory – some true. Sitting at this kitchen table, I can look out at the sundrenched patio, at the birdbath always filled with fresh, clean water, and the bench that no one sits on anymore, and I can talk about anything or nothing with equal emphasis.

It was here that I had told Alice about my dreams. About night after night of visiting memories I'd left so far behind me they seemed to belong to someone else. About learning to love the precocious, sun-bright child that had once been me.

I'd told her, too, about the darker dreams. Memories of pain and fear, like nights during the dark of the moon, less familiar than the brighter times, but coming always with a twinge of dread that the light might one day forget to come again.

Only one dream I have held back. That dream I have shared with no one except Rose.

Alice has told me her stories too, of when she and Glenn met. The first year of being "the secretary" and her fears that people would say of Glenn that he was the stereotypical "high powered executive who falls for his personal assistant who falls for his money."

Stories of moving into this very house back when the neighborhood was "not entirely acceptable." She'd hosted the parties, greeting Glenn's old friends at the door, then listening to them whisper when they didn't think she heard, or perhaps didn't care if she did, that "he'd come to his senses soon enough."

A country girl from Wisconsin, her family hadn't been wealthy. She hadn't been surprised that many of Glenn's friends were convinced she'd married him only for the security offered by his power, status, and hefty income.

But those friends weren't the ones who scrambled his eggs every morning, sprinkling in the finely chopped herbs and whipping the eggs until they were lemon colored and air filled. They weren't there to watch over him while he coughed, or to empty the trash when it filled with blood laden tissues.

Not only were those friends not there to sit with him when he lay unsleeping in the night, they didn't come in the day either. They sent cards and gifts, emails demanding updates, but none of his old corporate or society friends visited the house where they had once gathered for cocktails and fancy dinner parties.

It was David who came daily, who sat and read to Glenn until he slipped into restless sleep. David who would rise silently and leave the room, smile conspiratorially at Alice as he snagged a chocolate from the box of truffles sent by a well-intentioned friend who had no idea that Glenn could no longer digest such riches. David, who could be seen puttering among the roses, who would come in with a handful of fresh blooms to grace the bureau in Glenn's room.

And me. I come now too. I listen and learn while Glenn tells stories of taking over team after team, turning them from paranoid in-fighters prepared for corporate Armageddon, into fiercely loyal collaborators convinced that nothing could hold them back from creating the next Coca Cola.

And then there is the slender figure in red who trails behind me into the bedroom and settles at the foot of the bed, sitting cross legged or with tanned arms wrapped around her drawn up legs. He includes her in the conversations and teases her about not "worrying her pretty head about this grownup talk." But I notice he also watches her closely, and I can tell he takes stock in her reactions to his tales.

"They didn't mind insulting me in my own home," Alice said of their society friends. "I pretended I didn't notice, but Glenn overheard a comment one evening and threw everyone out. Every single person. Told them all to leave and to not expect to be invited again."

And he had held to his threat. They didn't stop the parties, but his high-society crowd wasn't invited. The guests became an eclectic mix of artists living in the area, college professors, shop owners, anyone they found interesting. Eventually a few of the old crowd filtered back in, those that Glenn trusted to add to the lively conversations without detracting from the spirit of equality he fostered in his home.

It was at one of these gatherings they first met David.

Now Alice and I watch David's lanky frame as he reaches to pull a greedy clematis vine off of a fence slat and twine it gently around the frame of a trellis. "I don't remember who he came with," she shakes her head ruefully. "I don't think we ever asked. He was just suddenly there, part of the group, in that quietly amused way of his. He didn't leave with whoever it was, I know that, because the sun came up and he and Glenn were the only two left talking. Right here at this table is where I found them the next morning."

She fumbles with the spoon in the honey jar. Glenn likes his tea sweet, the locally sourced honey is a fixture whenever Alice sets out the tea tray. I remember how my father used to mix softened butter with honey from a neighbor's hives and spread it thickly over fresh baked biscuits. I wonder if Glenn could digest biscuits.

"David is the only one of his friends that Glenn could tell about Beth Ann." She stops.

"It's a terrible thing," Alice's voice when she begins again is terse and tear clogged. "I understand why she left and took the girl. But I think surely she could forgive after all this time."

She means Glenn's ex-wife and his daughter, Beth Ann, estranged from him for nearly forty years. The girl had been only ten when her mother had packed their belongings into a friend's horse trailer and left for good. Glenn had come home to find the house nearly empty of furnishings and completely empty of his family.

The divorce had been finalized without their ever seeing each other again, an attorney hired by her parents appeared on his ex-wife's behalf, and he agreed to have no contact with the little Beth Ann as long as she was a minor.

David had told me that much, Alice has never mentioned it to me before. And I had never asked for details. I don't ask now.

Suddenly restless, Alice bustles over to the sink. The breakfast dishes that had been so unobtrusive until now require her full attention, and I know it's time for me to be elsewhere.

"I'm going to go sit with Glenn a bit, if you think he's up for company." I don't wait for a response. I carry my tea cup to the sink, pat her shoulder gently and take myself down the hall to the sunny space that had once been an executive's home office and is now his sick room.

"So what did you want to be when you grew up?" Glenn must be growing weary of talking; he wants to hear a story.

I curl my legs up into the oversized club chair. Rose perches on the chair arm, knees tucked under her chin, gaze never shifting from Glenn's face.

I gesture with my chin in her direction. "I wanted to be her." I'm half joking, half wistful.

"And I wanted to be Heidi, and the Girl of the Limberlost, and Rose in *Eight Cousins* or Mary in *The Secret Garden*. I guess those aren't grownups are they?

So…" I sort through memory files for something marked "when I grow up" and come up empty. Almost.

"I wanted to be a grand dame and hold salons where all the interesting people came and talked over cocktails and cigarettes until the sun came around again. I would have made a fantastic Grand Dame, don't you think? Or a madam!"

I expected him to laugh, instead he cocks his head slightly on the pillow and raises an eyebrow. "A madam?" he repeats. "Why not just be a whore?"

Almost, I'm offended.

Almost, I'm afraid that I've offended *him*.

"I don't romanticize prostitution," I assure him. "Not at all. But as I understand it, the madam ran a social club as much as she did a place where men came to buy sex. And I would have been very good at that, I suspect.

"On the other hand, the idea that having sex for money is a *crime*, but that having sex for status, for security, or just for a fancy dinner and night of dancing, is what any self-respecting person would do ... that makes no sense to me.

"By my definition, the truth is that any woman, or man, who has sex with someone for anything less than love of the other person is what you would call a 'whore.'" I use my fingers to indicate that I'm mentally putting that word in quotations.

"But somehow, our *story* is that sex for personal gain is acceptable if it is a socially recognized exchange like, 'You be my girlfriend, or even marry me, and have sex with me and I'll buy you pretty things and take you to dinner once a week.' And maybe both parties feel good about it and maybe they don't, but if they do, then everyone is happy because we have 'story' for it that makes it all right.

"But," I go on, "if both parties agree to a service and a price, and that service is sexual in nature, then our *story* is that it is wrong. Even if both parties feel like they got what they wanted and needed, our story is *still* that a wrong has been done.

"But I think it isn't *about* right or wrong, it's about the *story* we make up about it. In the end, the only right or wrong is *your* truth, what is right or wrong for *you*. And what is wrong for you can't be right for you to do to someone else. And what is wrong for someone else can't *really* be right for you either."

"So you're saying it isn't our place to judge?" His voice is flat, his brows are drawn tight.

"It isn't about judgment," I assert. "It isn't about whether it is our place, or our right. It just doesn't matter what we think or how we judge. Unless someone else accepts *our* judgment as part of *their* story, in which case the story has been changed because of what the *other* person chose to accept. They are just as free to discard it completely."

I feel creases between my eyebrows too. I know I'm not trying to convince him, I'm trying to explain to me. I glance often at the still figure next to me, but her eyes are still on his face. I can't depend on her to reflect truth back to me on this one.

I wrestle for words, a way to illustrate to him the knowing I am only now dragging into the light myself. Glenn is doing some wrestling of his own, I can tell by the way he picks at the bed cover. The way his gaze slips away from the two of us and focuses on the palate of color in the rose garden outside. The way a muscle in his jaw has started to twitch because he is clenching his teeth together so tightly.

That muscle twitch used to be one warning sign that my father was near to losing self-control. Time was, if I'd seen a man's jaw twitch that way I'd have either been girding for battle or high tailing it to the next county.

"Judgment is not only not my place," I clarify. "It isn't in my capacity."

He turns his head back toward me and I see with a start a glimmer of moisture in the corner of his eyes. "You mean that you leave that up to God? Judgment?"

"No. I leave it up to the other person. I can't possibly know their truth, what they came here to learn, or to teach, or to remember, or discover. For all I know, everyone who goes to war came here to learn something they could only learn by being part of a battle. Everyone who is sold into slavery, everyone who is killed in a natural disaster, everyone who commits murder or is murdered, they may have all come here to learn or teach a thing that requires that they take on that role. They came here to walk their own path, serve their own purpose. I am not in a position to judge their path or their purpose."

"So if you didn't know what you wanted to *be* when you grew up, did you know what you came here to *do*?"

"No. But I'm learning."

Without knowing what I'm going to say, I let the words tumble out; marbles spilling from a cosmic bag.

"I came here, to remember and to remind that violence, of words, of intentions, of spirit, is not our path.

"My role is not to judge the person, but to stop the behavior. Not to mete out vengeance, but to learn compassion.

"I came here to learn and teach and remember how to join together, not tear each other apart, how to let *truth* make us heart-whole.

"We cannot abuse one another without abusing ourselves, we cannot damage one another without damaging ourselves, and we cannot *heal* one another without healing ourselves. I came here to learn and teach and remember that we are one."

I'm channeling a voice that is not my own. The words are spirit driven. An oracle of self is speaking through me, and I wish someone were recording it. *This* is what my little red book should have told me. Imagine if I'd known all *this* at age fourteen!

"That is what I came here to learn and teach and remember and do. My choices might seem wrong to another person. But the choices I made make it *possible* for me to do what I came here to do. I choose," I stress it again for my own recognition, "to show compassion to all others, regardless of their acts, while doing all in my power to end their acts of violence, because violence harms the abuser as much as it does the victim. And to show the world that acts of violence, abuse, even war, are unnecessary and unattractive."

"Unnecessary and unattractive," Glenn's voice is harsh and thin. "That's the best you can come up with? Unnecessary and unattractive? What about wrong? What about a sin against God and nature? What about pure evil? I don't think 'unnecessary and unattractive' is going to stop people from going to war, or committing murder or rape."

I've stepped on a patch of emotional quicksand here, I feel it shifting under my feet.

"Don't you?" I never did have any sense about backing down from challenges. If I'm treading on quicksand I'll put a stake in it and hold on tight.

"Why *do* people go to war? If you boil it down, they either think there is something attractive enough to fight for, or they think it's necessary to preserve something they value.

"Same with murder, either they think the other person's death will achieve something they *do* want, or will protect them from something they *don't* want. Of course, that's all based on their belief and perception of what's attractive, what's necessary, what will be gained or what will be preserved. *Perception* is usually based on *deception.*"

I'm expecting Glenn to take issue with my treatise. He's not one to leave a stretch of sand unstaked either.

The muscle in his jaw is pulsing like a heartbeat. His eyes are closed. "What about rape?" The word comes at me, a whip cracking, the tip snaking toward me and connecting right between my eyes.

His lashing out is so physically painful I jerk my head back against the soft padding of the chair back. My first thought is, "How can he know?"

I look at the silent figure sitting on the chair arm, accusation in my eyes. But her brows are creased together, and she shakes her head at me. He doesn't know my story from her.

Tears are trickling from under Glenn's closed lids. Slowly he opens them. His eyes do not challenge or accuse, they plead. It comes to me that he did not snap that word at me because he knows my story, but because he needs me to interpret his own.

"Rape," I begin, feeling the words forming on my tongue, not birthed in my brain but in my heart. "I think rape is often an act of violence, a means to an end the same way that any other act of violence is perceived to be. Something to be gained, or something to be preserved. A path to false power, an illusion of power, but all acts of violence are that. Make it unattractive and unnecessary, show it as a false path, and there are those who will turn away from it."

"And when it isn't? When it isn't about power, or about gain or about preventing loss? What is rape then?"

Now my eyes are closed. Dots play again on the backs of my eyelids, a kaleidoscope of them, arranging and rearranging. I realize I'm seeing dots because I have stopped breathing. I fill my lungs.

The dots stop. Suddenly, ever so briefly, they form the outline of a rose.

"Sometimes," I say, without opening my eyes. "Sometimes it is about love."

I lift my gaze and meet his eyes. I register surprise and incredulous relief there, the afterimage of the rose superimposed on his features.

"It's still about desire, or preventing loss, but our society has confused desire with sex for so long and taught men that if they aren't man enough to take what they want that they will lose it, I think it's possible that they don't even realize that it's not sex that they desire, but love.

"There's no truth in that path because violence can never lead to love, but they follow the paths they're taught. Of course, they only get shame, not love, and that leads to more confusion and anger. It's what I meant about false paths to power and how we cannot damage one another without damaging ourselves, and we cannot *heal* one another without healing ourselves.

"But sometimes, if we keep our sights on what we seek, the true path appears. A path that takes us where we want to go, that lets us be the heroes we really are."

I find I am standing, although I don't remember pushing myself out of the chair.

"No," I correct myself. "Not sometimes, always. The true path always appears. It is up to us to walk it."

My feet take me from the room, down the hall, out the door, across the porch, and onto the path that wanders through the roses.

Stumbling a little, I listen for the near-silent sounds of David tending to his charges. I need him to tend to another charge.

He rises from under an arbor of pale pink roses. I register their bright apple green scent and tight whorled centers. Some part of me wants his voice, wants him to tell me something normal and unrelated to power and loss, wants to hear a love story that promises a happy ending.

"What's this one called?" I brush the tip of my nose against the center of a blossom, just to have a reason not to meet his eyes.

"This one's a sport, so it was bred from a bush variety. But it's been mutated to reach for the sky." Ask David to talk about roses and he always tells a love story. "It's called Alchymist. Look at the way the blossoms change color as they open, from rosy pink, to golden, to creamy white. Just like a woman's

160

skin – from a baby's rosy blush to a girl's golden glow to the matron's pale cheek. Beautiful in every stage of life."

He waits patiently for me to take my face out of the rose and meet his eyes.

"Glenn needs you." I blurt out. "I've upset him, and he needs you."

He nods, asks no questions. He pulls off his gardening gloves and brushes a bit of hair off my forehead with one finger. "Hmm," he presses his lips together slightly. "Looks like you've upset the two of you. I'll let you talk to the Alchymist here, I'll go and sit with Glenn."

As quickly and quietly as that, he's gone. I look at the sky through the veil of rose and wrought iron trellis, black, green and pink patterns against a perfect backdrop of blue. I remember the day I met David, "Oh I'm a climber, no doubt about it. Gotta get up above everything, see over walls and peek through fences. You'll find me nodding down at you from way up there. But my roots stay grounded. Always."

I am grateful for his roots.

When I can breathe without crying I go back to the kitchen table. Alice is sitting with a fresh pot of tea, a cooking magazine open next to her cup.

I fetch a clean cup from the rack next to the range and fill it from the pot. It had been warm under the rose arbor, but the heat from the cup still feels good in my hands, and the steam that rises at the first sip soothes the tight muscles in my face.

"Alice," I begin, sitting next to her. Her gaze shifts to me, I can tell she's been far away; with no party to plan for, the glossy pictures of gourmet fare can't hold her attention.

"I know that Beth Ann's mother took Beth Ann when she left and made Glenn promise not to contact her while she was a minor. David told me that much of the story." I put my hand on Alice's arm. "Has he ever heard from her?" I ask. "Would she know how to reach him?"

"She won't. Ever. He raped her."

She says it flatly. My fingers freeze over her wrist. I suppose I should have guessed. I suppose, at some level, I had.

"I know what you're thinking. How I could love a man who would rape his daughter, right? That's what you're thinking, isn't it? You know, he couldn't understand that either. He nearly wouldn't let me love him. He could not believe that once I knew what he had done I wouldn't run away from him the way she did. And then he did wonder if I only loved his money, he was so sure that I could not possibly love him."

Her words are a torrent now, having said "rape," having gotten that one word out loud into the sunshine, the dam is broken.

"But I do love him, whatever he did then, and still I can't believe that he did that, I love the man I met, the man I married, the man he is. I don't know who he was when he did that terrible thing, but I know Glenn, and he is not a monster."

Her eyes beg me to understand, to forgive her for loving against reason, to forgive him for something he might have done in another lifetime, to show her a way to reconcile the loving with the transgression.

"Love is a sticky thing," I move my hands to my cup, and she puts both of hers over her eyes, resting her face in her palms like children do when they don't want to see the scene they know is coming in a horror picture show.

"We attach all kinds of things to it." I'm not sure if I'm talking to Alice or to myself, or if I'm just filling space with the exploration of an idea. "We need, we call it love. We want, we call it love. Sometimes we fear even, and call it love. And we try to get love by forcing people to need us, to want us, or even to fear us. But need and want and fear – that's not love, and it won't inspire love.

"Love is like one of those fly strips. We stick all kinds of things to it, but they are still what they are. They're still flies – just dead ones."

I hear a startled chuckle come, all unwilling, from behind her hands.

"We cannot turn need or want or fear into love, any more than a fly can become one with that fly strip. We can stick all those other emotions to love, but we'll still be without love. That doesn't keep us from trying. Rape can be like that." I hear my voice echoing what I said to Glenn, "sometimes it is an act of love."

"Rape. An act of love. How?"

Faced with the same thought, her face is a mirror of Glenn's. Surprise and incredulous relief. Again I see the outline of the rose, something seen in bright sunlight and imprinted forever on the retina of my mind.

"Because, sometimes, love is what is sought. Perhaps even what is given in the end. Not in the act, that is an evil, evil thing and never right for the abuser or the abused, but in the intent." It's time to tell her of that one dream, the one I'd never shared.

I swallow hard, remind myself to breathe, and begin the story. I don't start with the night my father came to my room. I start with a picture of the golden child perched high on her father's shoulder, one plump arm wrapped securely around his neck.

I tell her about my early years, hours and days spent in the cab of an eighteen wheeler with the North American Van Lines logo on its side, crossing the country pulling households behind us. Stories I've heard told again and again about that bright spirit, though I'm only now learning to recognize that spirit as myself.

I show her the child who wanted to hug the sea, horrifying the adults on the beach, who'd pretty much forgotten about me until they saw me running toward the waves lapping at the sand. When my mother finally caught up to me she says she heard me saying, "No, no, no, no." Over and over, "no," but still moving without pause toward the incoming tide.

I show her the hellion riding bareback, skinnying up tree trunks, walking fence rows and turning cartwheels in the pasture, dress flying unheeded over my head as I tumbled over the fescue.

I show her the book worm, sneaking novels to bed, recruiting neighborhood kids to act out stories on the concrete bridge that spanned our overflow ditch, memorizing poems and finally writing my own stories and poems, hiding them in drawers and between my mattress and box springs.

"So you see, I was strong-minded, even as a baby," I tell Alice. She's laughing finally at the picture of me running the doting adults ragged with my willful antics. I realize that underlying her chuckle is the rich tone of the grand piano in the conservatory.

Once I tune an ear to it, I know I've been hearing the notes for a while, it's woven into the fabric of what I remember saying. Now it embarks on a different melody. Simple sequence of opening notes, ta, da da, da, da, da, and repeat.

Without getting up to look, I see the figure at the keyboard. Slim straight back draped in red and molasses gold hair. Only she would know the soundtrack of my joys and sorrows, she's been playing a medley to smooth my way into the story I'm bracing myself to tell.

I can't tell if Alice hears the notes, if she does they aren't registering on her face. But they aren't played for Alice. This tapestry of song is for me.

"I think when I was little, I might have been 'Daddy's girl.' But as I got older, my father became more distant. He didn't hug me anymore, and the rules changed. It wasn't cute when I smarted off, it was bad. It wasn't funny when I ran wild with the goats and chickens, it was unladylike.

"When I was six, he beat me with a pear switch. When I was eight he raped me."

There. It's out, the word lying yet again in the sunshine that drapes the kitchen table. If I expected the recoil I'd seen when I'd told Vincent about that other beating, I didn't get it. Alice only nods, waiting for the rest.

I give it to her. I paint for her the five years of never knowing, dreading the next visit to my room.

I paint for her too, the hunger for approval, for safety, for love, even the sense of fear and loss when he did not come to my room again.

"Of course," she says in answer to my story. "Of course, you craved his approval and affection whatever way you could get it. Little girls need to be loved."

"Oh no," I'm quick to correct her. "I always had love. I never doubted that during those five years. Only after."

"I suppose, you believed what you needed to believe," Alice's voice is soft with pity.

"No," I correct her yet again. "I believed what my heart told me was true. After, I stopped hearing my heart and listened to my pride, to my fear, to my reason, and to all the stories of other people's truth. Then I was deceived.

"You see, I tried to turn all that needing and wanting and fearing into love, and I couldn't see love. I tried to understand the violence and the sex in the context of wanting and needing and fearing, and I couldn't see love. But I knew in my heart the love was there. Somewhere.

"I became blind with all that wanting and needing and fearing. Then I forgot that I was loved.

"After I started telling myself my story the way other people would see it. After I started seeing myself as a helpless victim, as damaged goods, as a slave to his temper and my mother's fear. *Then* I began to think that no one loved me.

"When I told my story the way I thought everyone else would tell it, I believed that no one loved me, no one would ever love me, because I did not deserve love. That was my perception, what I chose to believe. But that truth wasn't taking me anywhere I wanted to go."

I hear an echo of what I'd said to Glenn, "Perception is usually based on deception," I repeat it for her.

"Our hearts, our very souls, know what is true," I add, "But we insist on seeing with our minds."

Alice's head shakes back and forth in disbelief. I doubt she even realizes she is moving.

My throat hurts from fighting emotion, words burning their way from my heart to my mouth. "Alice," I lean forward, vaguely registering the opening notes of *All Through the Night*, coming into the silence between her name and the rest of what I have to say.

"Alice, the things we do in the name of love, those things may not be true expressions of love, may even be horrible perversions of love, but it doesn't mean the love isn't there. My father did not beat me or rape me out of love, but he did do those things out of a desire for love. And he did love me. Always."

"How?" That word is all she can articulate for several seconds. I let them tick, listening with one part of my mind to the sweet notes from the piano and the trill of birdsong from the garden.

"How could he possibly think that would make you love him?"

"How do you define love?" It isn't an answer, not even a question I expect her to answer. But a question I know I will have to answer for myself.

"I think he defined love as obedience. As compliance. As subservience even. He needed to break me to his will in order to believe that I loved him. Of course, none of those definitions of love really express love. Nor can love be forced the way you can force obedience or sex. But he acted from his belief. And he lived long enough to *change* what he believed, and to change his behavior accordingly. I am thankful that I was there for that."

Alice's face is still incredulous. "So that makes it all okay?" she challenges. "You don't hold him accountable for what he did to you? No one should have stopped him? There is no price for him to pay? You suffered all that, and because he changed, you just forgive him? How? Are you just waiting for karma to kick in and balance everything out?"

"Oh, Alice, it isn't forgiveness. I tried that. But to forgive required me to judge and it felt so arrogant, something given from a superior to an inferior. I forgave, but it felt false, and it wasn't ever enough.

"And no, I can't say it's all okay. Nor can I say what should have happened. Believing that even the most violent acts can be committed out of love or a desire for love, doesn't mean I condone violent acts. I'm certainly not saying that there should be no prevention and no consequences. We need prevention and consequences as much for the sake of those who commit violent acts as for the people they harm.

"And karma will balance everything, but it's not instant and I don't think it's about punishment. It's just balance, and his karma is none of my concern. The only karma I can change is mine.

"So maybe I was best served by going through my experience exactly the way I did. I believe that is true because it brought me here, and I don't know what joy I might have missed, or what sorrow I might have suffered, if my life had taken another path.

"But really, Alice. Who would I hold accountable? My parents? Their parents? The community? Who do I blame for the conditioning, for all the things that we stick to love, that aren't love? How far back do I go to find the root of the need and the want and the fear? It's not given to me to judge them as people. It's certainly not my place to forgive anyone, or hold them accountable for how they handle their search for love. I can only be accountable for how I handle my own.

"Wow!" She sits back in her chair, and I am surprised to note that the distance she puts between us by doing so stings.

"Just wow. I'm impressed, but I don't understand. Not at all."

"Alice, you mentioned all the things I 'suffered.' You treat my story like a tragedy. You think I was helpless because I was 'only a child.' But I know that I am the resilient spirit I am *because* I had those experiences and accepted it as part of the lesson I came here to learn and to teach.

"You think I didn't have any control? I know that I was very much in control. If I had been willing to break to his will, if I had cried and begged him, the beating would have stopped. But my role was not only to be true to my own spirit, it was also to force him to find another path to earn my love, a truer path. And he did.

"You think I couldn't have stopped him from raping me? I tell you if I had made one peep, if I had told one soul, he would have stopped. But my role was to force him to find another way of expressing his love. And he did.

"You think it wasn't worth it? I still don't know the extent of the power I have available to me because of those choices. I still don't know what kind of mountains I'm going to move. But I know this," my voice drops, my throat is constricting even as my heart expands.

"My parents weren't monsters. They were souls who came to experience and learn just as I did. They had their role, I had mine. They chose their demons to battle, I chose mine. Sometimes we won, sometimes we lost. Just like every other person."

She isn't convinced. "Not every other person abuses a child. Or stands by and watches it done. Beth Ann's mother did the right thing, I just wish Beth Ann could find it in her heart to forgive."

I'm not getting through. She cannot see my bright, clear vision of interconnectivity, of all of us playing out our roles of abused and abuser, of monster and victim in order to learn that we are none of us one or the other, but all of us one and the same.

She doesn't understand that this is exactly why we are born, souls free to fly, choosing to ground ourselves in the fallacy of human limitations. We choose, so that we might have the joy of finding our way to oneness again and again.

The knowing of it is washing through me, an electrical current humming the melody that is the original for every other song. She can't feel the peace and bliss she is missing by clinging to definitions of right/wrong, love/hate, perception/reality that keep her cadged in isolation.

"Perhaps most people can say they have never abused a child." I start again from a different direction.

"But how many of us can say we have never abused anyone?" I remember my angry words to Vincent, I hadn't known then what I was trying to say, now I do.

"Can any of us say we have never struck out at one weaker than ourselves? Never yelled at someone who couldn't defend themselves? I'll bet almost everyone has done that. Isn't that abuse?

"Perhaps we can say we have never stood aside while a child was beaten or even seen the bruises and done nothing, but can any of us say we have never let a wrong go by and looked the other way?

"Haven't you ever condemned someone as unreasonable or unacceptable? How do you know they aren't battling their demons? Do you stop to wonder about their fears, their pains, or what abuse they have endured with no one to take their part?

"Some turn their pain outward, some turn it inward, but if we judge the person, we only augment the pain and validate the feelings of worthlessness and unfairness and hopelessness that breed abuse. We must stop abuse, for the sake of both the participants.

"To me, forgiveness was actually a barrier to healing, because it was based on a premise of blame and wrongness. Forgiveness created a debt and a distance. What I needed was compassion, understanding that we're all in it together, we are all, in truth, one."

She's unmoved. "Dixie, it sounds good. But it doesn't make sense. I know you mean 'we are one' in the spiritual sense. But here on earth there are bad people who do bad things to people like you who don't deserve it. It's sad. But it's true."

I consider reminding her that she has just implied that Glenn, the man she has loved for most of her adult life, is one of those bad people. I don't.

"We are one because we have all been abused, and we have all been the abuser. We all need to receive the gift of compassion, and we all need the gift of having compassion for others.

"Compassion doesn't condone the acts, or even pardon the abuser. Compassion isn't based on understanding the cause or judging the worth of someone's suffering, but simply understands that the suffering is real just as our own suffering is real. Compassion looks to relieve the suffering of all – abused and abusers alike. Compassion allowed me to condemn the acts without despising the person. Compassion left me room for love."

I can tell my conviction frightens her, it even frightens me a little bit.

"Alice," I begin again, working to relax the grip passion has on my throat, soften my voice to a cajoling whisper. "I do *not* say that there should be no consequences for abuse. Violence against another is always a call for us to intervene. If we ignore the abused, we leave the abuser to drown in their pain just as surely as we do those that they abuse. But," I plead with my eyes for her to hear me, "but, if we condemn the abuser we create more abuse. Only when we choose compassion for abused and abuser alike can we hope to stop the cycle."

What was it I said to Glenn? It comes back to me, lines of a poem I might have learned before I could speak, waiting to be called up again.

"We cannot abuse one another without abusing ourselves. We cannot damage one another without damaging ourselves. And we cannot heal one another without healing ourselves." I speak it aloud, an invocation.

The piano is still. I imagine I can hear the motes of dust dancing in the sunlight above the oak surface of the table. My breath comes hard inside my lungs, my heart is taking up so much space in my chest there is no room for them to expand.

Her voice, when it comes, is thin and tiny. I have to lean close to hear her words.

"How do we heal? How do we heal one another?"

I'm tempted to say, "How the heck would I know?" The person I was last month might well have said just that. But the person I was last month hadn't sat at this kitchen table, wrapped her hands around a cold tea cup for warmth and said into the sunlight, "When I was eight he raped me."

The person I've become answers. "We love."

It's anticlimactic after my passionate monologue. But the truth of it reverberates to my fingertips and toes.

"You know, for years I never told anyone about any of it. Not even the bruises, certainly not the black eyes and broken nose, and never, ever the rape."

For the third time that word is placed between us in the light.

My talk with Vincent some weeks ago comes back to me again, more clearly than I could articulate it at the time.

"I don't want people to see me as a victim because I'm not. I don't even want them to see me as a survivor – like that's something special? We are all of us survivors. The story most people hear when they hear my story isn't what I want people to associate with me. It isn't how I want to connect with people. Because it is not me.

"I am not defined by what others think of me, but by what I believe of myself. My story isn't what has been done to me, my story is what I have done, who I have become. My story is not one of abuse or survival. It's the same as anyone's story, it's the story of the transformation of me then, to me now.

"I am who I choose to be. Always. And you know what? Me now is pretty glad to be me." I think about the rose, the Alchymist, transforming from blush to pale as the bloom matures.

I know, although I do not try to say it to her now, I am the alchemist behind my own transformation. Others may add ingredients, apply heat and force, but I am the only one who can direct the outcome.

"Because you forgave him? You forgave your mother and all the people who didn't do anything? That's the transformation?"

"Alice. It wasn't forgiveness. It wasn't even the compassion, although that opened the door. It was just love.

"We love. It becomes our truth. And through that truth, we become whole."

We sit in silence. My hands still wrapped around a cold tea cup, hers clenched, fingers intertwined. The clock in the foyer chimes the half hour, one rich gong. That clock had belonged to Alice's family. The clock, the piano, and this kitchen table were the only pieces of furniture she had brought to their marriage.

I wonder what I have left to offer her. What gift of words will reach her, caught as she is in her own story? What truth do I have left that will let her understand the transformative power of love?

Instead she offers the gift to me. "He loved," her lips form a half smile as she gazes out on her tomato plants and herbs, the roses making a color-streaked backdrop behind them.

"It started with the checks. No one knew about them. But right before I gave up being his personal assistant, I was organizing all the accounts. He'd put a check stub from his personal account in the file by accident.

"I asked him what to do with it and he got flustered. It was the first time, one of the only times, he ever snapped at me, so I knew he was upset. It made me curious," Alice colors slightly and I see a hint of the shy young woman she had been, admitting any curiosity about her employer would likely have been a bold choice for her.

"So I looked up the organization. It was a shelter for women and children, victims of domestic violence. I was puzzled, but right after that I was transferred to a new department and we started dating, kind of. He asked me to a charity dinner, a charity the company supported, not the shelter. Then he stopped by my desk a couple of nights later and asked if I had dinner plans. I was already in love. It was a dream, and I didn't want to risk waking up. So I didn't ask any more questions."

Her twinkle is coming back as her story burns through her fear and sorrow.

"After a while I remembered that check. I wanted so much to show him how I could fit into his life, how I could care for something for his sake. I didn't have money to contribute, I was still a glorified secretary. But I thought I might volunteer. So I went there.

"They gave me a tour of the home. One room, it used to be the dining room I think, they used for a playroom and library. We stopped in the doorway and there he was. He was sitting cross-legged on the rug, kids stretched out all around. His hair was mussed and standing on end. I'd never seen him so relaxed. I almost spoke, but something stopped me."

Alice turns to me, back to this moment, at this table, connecting again with the man she still loves beyond reason. "It wasn't a coincidence really," she shrugs. "There was one night a week we never saw each other. I'd always thought he must have a standing 'boys night out' that he didn't want to tell me about. So that was the night I was free to go to the shelter and ask about volunteering. I never went back, that belonged to Glenn."

Her hands are unclasped, she's using them to tell her story now, gesturing as she talks. "He told me about the shelter when he told me about Beth Ann. It was where her mother went first when she discovered what he'd done. After I took over managing the household accounts, I realized his donations pretty much kept it open, but they loved him most for his way with the kids. He really listened to them; they trusted him to always be straight with them, but kind.

"He volunteered there almost every week until he was so sick he couldn't stay out of bed even for an hour at a time. It's in his will; this house and a trust fund will go to them so they can care for more kids." She smiles. "I like thinking of this house finally being full of little ones. We never had any."

I had thought my heart had expanded to fill all the available space my ribs had to offer, I was wrong. I feel it swelling into my throat, pushing tears into my eyes. I sit listening to everything she isn't saying into the silence after that last sentence.

"He was afraid, after he told me the story about Beth Ann, that I would think he wanted to be around the children because…" her voice trails away. Again, I know what she isn't saying. "I would never have believed that was why. It started as penance. But he kept going out of love."

"You're right," she traces a circle onto the table between us. "We love. We heal. We become whole."

The silence now is a comfortable one of nothing-more-needs-to-be-said. We smile into each other's eyes, fellow travelers arrived together in Eden. I remember a page in my little red book,

We try to define heaven, when what we want is a better earth.

We've just created it. A better earth.

The entire house is quiet except for a rustle from the hallway. For several seconds the noise doesn't register, for another second my mind cannot make sense of it. Then I place it, the sound of wheels moving over a hardwood floor. Glenn.

Like rewinding a movie to watch a scene I've missed, I see David standing in the hallway. He would have heard us talking and, in that eerie magical way he had, he would have known that Glenn needed to hear what was coming.

I can just see him lifting Glenn into the wheelchair, usually only brought out when Glenn had an appointment with his oncologist. If anyone else had tried to get Glenn to comply without question, the discussion would have been heard in the next county. But David would have just said, "Let's go" and Glenn would have replied, "Okay, let's."

They must have been listening from the hallway. For how long?

In my head I hear David's voice, "Let's go."

I hear myself answer aloud, "Okay, let's."

Without thinking, I stand, pushing my chair back. Alice stands too, a question on her face.

"Let's go see about Glenn," I finish the sentence with the first thing that comes to mind.

"Oh," she's suddenly the nurse. "It's time I got his meds down him and maybe he'll eat a little bit. At least a shake." As she speaks, she's crossing to the refrigerator, pulling out a canned meal replacement "shake" and pouring it into a crystal goblet. It does look a little more appetizing served that way, although I can't imagine that Glenn is any more fond of sipping it from crystal than he would be from a plastic cup. Armed with the meal in a goblet and a saucer of capsules and tablets, Alice moves toward the hallway.

David is just coming out as we reach the door to Glenn's room. His eyes meet mine, a tacit suggestion. "I think I've tired Glenn enough for one day," I say. "I'd like to sit in the sun for a few minutes, then I need to be getting home."

David's light voice comes in right behind mine, "I'm going to have to go soon as well, but I need to gather up some clippings and put some tools away first. I'll come in and say goodbye in a bit." He winks at Alice, and together we head back toward the French doors and the sunshine.

Faintly, I hear a scale being played on the piano, nimble fingers running lightly over the keys. As we open the door to the garden, I hear the beginning of a gentle lullaby.

These days are definitely the dog days of summer, so hot that even the dogs lag on their leashes along the paths in the park. The only time of day worth walking in is before the sun climbs high enough to broil the sidewalks and anyone daring to venture onto them.

Vincent's training schedule hasn't changed, but he's relying on the hated treadmill or stationary bike to get his cardio in most days. I try to deny the faint relief I feel at having justification for not walking and talking about everything except the thing we're both thinking about.

Not that we ever walk in silence. Vincent gives me a running commentary of his fights, his projects, his plans for the soon-to-begin semester of college classes, his on-again-off-again relationship with a woman half again his age and a good four inches taller who knocked his socks off while scoring a knock-out in the ring. She'd just moved to the city, and they shared a trainer and undeniable chemistry but seemingly not a lot of anything else. Sheena, he'd declared more than once, was either the best thing to ever happen to him or the worst. He wasn't sure which. It depended on the day.

It's been two weeks, maybe more, since we shared a walk. I'd pulled my night owl self out of bed at an alarmingly early time to meet him. Already the air is heavy and humid even though it hasn't rained in recent memory. From the car I'd seen the roadside grasses showing swathes of brown, while the mighty Mississippi, only a couple of miles away, is low along its banks and the pool in the grotto where we agreed to meet for our walks is sluggish with an oily film on its surface. Rain is in the forecast today and I'm hoping it breaks this oppressive heat wave as well as my less-than-bubbly temperament.

He's late. Which is not like him. Usually I'm the one running on "Dixie

Time" which has a plus or minus variable of five to ten minutes.

I watch a family of ducks glide under the arched bridge, hugging the mossy banks, dunking bills in the water from time to time or suddenly upending themselves so that the points of their tail feathers aim for the sky. The adage about early birds seems to apply to waterfowl as well.

I've waited maybe 20 minutes and I'm wondering if I've mistaken the day or time we'd agreed to meet when I hear footsteps behind me. I look, even though I'm sure it isn't him, the dragging, weary step can't be my friend.

But it is. He's dressed for running, baggy shorts and tank, high top trainers on his feet. His face and body tell another tale. I've seen him on training days after a tough fight, bruised and once with stitches across his temple, and he looked more ready to train then than he does now.

"Vincent," I gasp taking a tentative step in his direction. "What happened, are you okay?"

He waves me back, then jerks his head toward the trail that leads up to the paved path. "Sorry." The word is taut between us. "I should have called, but I forgot. Just left the hospital."

"Then what are you doing here?" I ask. "Why were you in the hospital? Should you even be training today?" Questions beat at me, but I'm having to hustle to catch up to his retreating back. Clearly, he's healthy enough to set a pace I'm not prepared to keep, and he's agitated enough not to notice or care.

"Not me," he snaps back over his shoulder. "Had to take Sheena."

"Who did she fight?" I ask, assuming the injury was the result of a match. "How bad is it?"

"It's bad. They admitted her. Her old man showed up. Her ex," he adds, "not her dad. She hasn't seen *him* in ages."

I've caught up with him now, but not because he slowed down for me. I had to jog along the sidewalk to finally reach his side and I'm short of breath trying not to let him pull ahead of me again. I'm sorting through his words, gathering that it was Sheena's father who had been missing from her life for ages and her ex-husband who had arrived on the scene and wreaked so much damage that Sheena was now in the hospital. But whether he was upset because a woman he cared for had been assaulted, because he'd had to see her that way, because he had to leave her to keep a commitment to me, or all or none of the above, I could only guess.

I reach out to him, still having to extend my arm forward as he's gotten ahead of me again and grab his elbow. "Stop a sec," I say, trying not to let my lack of breath color my voice. "Why are you here? Does she need you? Would you rather be with her?"

Mercifully he stops, standing with his feet planted wide, arms crossed on his chest, gaze weary but defiant. For the first time since we met, I feel challenged, even threatened, and it is a conscious effort not to mirror his stance.

"I keep my promises." He states it flatly, but clearly there is more. I nod, silently.

"I wasn't going to even tell you," he continues. "I know you're going to give me all your high-and-mighty spiritual bullshit about forgiveness and love, and you don't know what it's like to have some evil monster on your trail showing up and beating you senseless then just taking what he wants, what men want, while you're just lying there bleeding and crying. You wouldn't know a thing about that, and I wasn't going to tell you, or I wouldn't have come."

His chin juts a little harder on that last line, his nostrils flare and I can see the red in his eyes is as much from fighting tears as from lack of sleep. There is a fissure line inside him, and he's got one foot on either side of it as it gets wider and wider.

"That's why she moved here, you know. To try to get away from him. And she learned to box so she could defend herself. Except he figured out where she was and showed up while she was in the shower, and she didn't even get in one punch. Not. One. Punch." He punches the air in front of him, snarling, seeing the face of a man he's never met as the punch connects, shattering bone and everything that is horrid and cruel and loveless about the world.

I feel tears on my cheeks watching him, remembering that helpless, hopeless feeling of not being able to turn back time and of knowing we are powerless to change the outcome even if we could go back to the beginning of the nightmare and start it over again.

"So," he says, dropping his piercing eyes to glare into my face. "I suppose you're going to tell me she should just turn the other cheek, the one he didn't fracture, that is, and forgive him and forgive all the stupid authority types who were supposed to keep him away from her, and that everything will just be okay? Because I'm not telling her that, I'm not a liar. I'm not going to tell her *anything* is going to be okay."

I reach out to touch his arm, but he jerks away. I swallow hard and tuck my hand back into the crook of my other elbow. My mind starts to formulate a dozen thousand sentences but none of them say anything that matters. Finally, I ask him, "What would you like to do, Vincent?"

"I'd like to kill the son of a bitch." His fists tighten as he speaks, the corded muscles jump in his biceps and along his forearms. His face tightens too, the left corner of his lip lifts and I see a fleeting glimpse of his teeth, startlingly white against the darkness of his skin.

"I've never wanted to kill anybody before," he adds, "but him. He's no good living, and she's better off if he's dead."

In my thoughts I acknowledge the truth of that. Quite likely Sheena is safer at least, if this man is no longer alive to threaten her. But I know the sequence of emotions that often tumble down when that one domino is overturned. Guilt, because somehow we should have handled ourselves differently, or even shame at being glad of someone else's death. Anger, that so much of our lives have been stolen and we were powerless to stop the theft. Fear, that there are other monsters in human form, and we won't know them until we've seen the damage done for ourselves. So, would she be better off? I doubt it, but this is not the time to say what I think.

I can see too, that this primal need to counter violence with greater, more definite violence, is challenging Vince's worldview as surely as my truth of compassion and healing had done. Until this summer he'd walked a charmed path through an often-violent landscape believing he was under the protective umbrella of a god who would only show him what he asked to see. He'd believed violence was a controlled game, with a system of rules and points, wins and losses, and a running invitation to come back and do it again next week.

In his personal story, people who were violent outside of that system were monsters. He would never meet those monsters because that wasn't what he asked to see in the world. But now he was face-to-face with something he never asked to see, his mind filled with violence that had no place in the system of wins or losses, feeling a powerlessness he'd probably never felt before in his life.

And he was face-to-face with me.

"Vincent, I'm so sorry." It's a banal thing to say, but it is true. "But being the cause of another human's death is a hard thing to bring on yourself. You have so much to offer, to Sheena and to the world. I hope you won't let another man's choices dictate your future."

His jaw drops, "That's all you have to say?" He spits out the words. "Really? What happened to the wise woman knows everything about abuse and trauma and, I don't know, everything?" He's waving his arms at me now, punctuating his words until he finishes with something between a shout and a gasp.

"I never said I knew everything about anything," my patience is gone, I spit words right back at him. "I said I learned the truth about my story, not that I know the truth about your story, or Sheena's story, or anyone else's story. That's the whole point, isn't it, that we choose our truth, and I can't choose for her or for you. Hell, I'm just now discovering that I have the power to even choose for myself. But if you choose a story where no one is safe until someone else is dead, you're going to end up with a lot of blood on your hands!"

My hands are on my hips now, my stance as wide as his, my face as tight as the face in front of me. The biggest difference is that my tears are flowing freely while he's still holding his in by sheer force of will and shame.

We lock eyes like that for one beat, two, and then so many beats that my heart feels like it must break out of the prison of my chest if it is to go on beating any longer.

Finally, he blinks, stands straighter, drops his arms to his sides. My heart eases for a second, but then he draws in a deep breath and in a thin, tight voice says, "Don't talk to me, don't call me, don't text me. Ever. Just do the world a favor and go to hell."

He turns his back and walks a few steps, breaks into a trot, then into a flat-out run. I watch him getting smaller through a haze of tears only to realize that not all the moisture on my face is salty. The predicted rain has begun to fall.

I'm still standing on the path, rain that would have been so welcome yesterday mingling with the tears on my cheeks and already forming puddles on the sidewalk. Gradually I become aware that I'm not alone anymore. Rose is sitting motionless on the bench next to the path, her hair plastered to her head and shoulders as though she were as solid as any other human child. I step off the sidewalk, my running shoes squishing a little, and sit next to her.

"He doesn't understand," I say.

"No," she agrees. "He can't."

I remember something Vincent said the first day we met, a day as wet as this one but with the cool freshness of an earth being reborn instead of today's bucket of water dumped on a fire and brimstone preview of the underworld. He'd said, "I figure God is good. He ain't gonna introduce me to any bad people." Now that he'd been confronted by people whose actions caused immeasurable harm, he was refusing to see that even in the light of this knowledge his God was no less good, and people were no more bad than they had been when his cheerful faith been unchallenged.

"Can't, or won't?" I ask, bitterness seeping through. "He won't even try, won't even discuss this, won't even listen. You know it's not like I have all the answers, but I know this: if violence is the answer, then we've sure as hell misunderstood the question."

"That's good! You should write that in the book."

"What book?" I ask, confused and irritated by the change in direction and her tone of voice. "I'm serious here, he's so smart but he's just refusing to see what's true. What does that have to do with a book?"

"Your red book," she prods me. "It has lines, for you to write on, but you've never added anything of your own. You should write that in that book."

I raise my eyebrows, thinking back along the lines of our voices and thoughts but still only seeing Vincent's confusion, pain, and stubbornness.

I can hear the quotations as she repeats my words, as though she were inscribing them into the little red book through the power of her voice.

"If violence is the answer, then we have misunderstood the question."

"Ah," I acknowledge her words, but there is no responding excitement or agreement.

Silence follows. Each of us tracking our own thoughts, I suppose. That's what I'm doing anyway. Tracking my thoughts, following Vincent, seeing him pounding the bags, pounding his sparring partner, pounding his head against a wall he cannot see or define but that confines him no matter which way he turns. Once we have come face-to-face with violence, we must either come to terms with its existence or lose ourselves in fighting or avoiding it until we die or surrender.

I see my thoughts lining up in binaries. This or that. If not that, then only this. Two choices for everything and no door number three. Like a decision tree with every line branching into two options and everything else a dead end. The human brain defaults to binaries, black or white, right or wrong, good or bad, safe or threatened, dead or alive, human or monster.

I look at Rose, at her calm face, the jaw set firmly even as the eyes are soft and seeing into a future beyond my lifetime or comprehension. "You can choose." I hear her voice in my head, but it is the voice of memory, she's not sharing her thoughts with me in this moment.

We choose. We create our lives though choosing. I'd said as much to Vincent. And surely our choices didn't come to a this or that, black or white, right or left path. In every fork in the road there are still multiple choices, it's just that only two of them are paved.

Sometimes the thing we most want has no path already paved that leads to it. We don't take the road less traveled, we choose the direction that has never been traveled, carving our path through meadows and swamps and forests unchallenged for so long that there is no navigation for us to follow except that bright light of a choice that pulls us ever onward.

I may have been thinking to myself, but as usual, Rose is privy to what comes of my thinking. "So how will you choose your path then," she asks.

"I guess I already have," I answer without pausing to examine my thoughts. "I've chosen to live by my truth, what feels true in every piece of me: that we're all one, we're all divine, we're all playing our part consciously or not. We're all here to create a life, an experience, and our reasons for choosing any experience are as individual as we are. I must live by that or it's not living. I haven't found that path, but I'm making one. When I stray from that path, I feel it. And it hurts."

She nods. More silence, broken only by the occasional ping of a water drop as it loosens itself from the branch above and lands on the thin metal of an abandoned soda can lying under the tree.

"Actually," I continue as though there had not been several breaths and pings in between one thought and the next, "it's that light. That light I must follow that determines the path I choose. That's our true choice, I think, the choice of where we want to be, at the end of the day, or the adventure, or the life, or eternity. We create our life by choosing, but I think we also create our world, our reality. We don't all live in the same world. Vincent doesn't even live in the same world today as he did yesterday. He's creating his world through his choices and the world he's creating today hurts."

"Yes," she agrees. "He's choosing pain right now, and perhaps that choice will eventually lead him to his own light. But what choice will you make?"

Running just under the surface of her words I hear the reminder. I'm not the creator of anyone else's choices, or their lives. My choices are the only ones I have the power to make. Vincent will follow his path, and maybe it will meet mine again, or maybe the memory of the path I shared with him will bring him back to his own truth and I will never know. But at this fork in the road, I have a choice. Either honor his choice to never see me again or defy it. Which choice would take me to my own light?

There, I realized, was that binary choice again. One point in time, right now, branching into two options for the next step. What happened to the cardinal rule of improv, never either/or, always yes/and? How could I do both, honor my truth and his choice?

"Do you know what I realized," Rose's voice fits into my reverie like a key in a lock. "When you shut me out and refused to see me or hear me, when you wouldn't open your mind to me at all? I learned something then."

She's not looking into the distant future anymore, she's turned her body toward mine on the bench to look into my eyes when they meet hers, eyebrows raised, inviting her silently to share the rest of her discovery.

"I heard it so plainly," she continues. "I thought at first it was you thinking it, but I couldn't feel your mind, so it came from another source. But I heard this, 'You can still hold in your heart those you cannot hold in your life.'"

"That's what I did, you know," she continued. "You were always in my heart, and I was in yours. And that's what brought me back to you out there in Kansas, your heart opened just enough that the part of you in my heart could feel the part of me in your heart and they had to come together. Like we'd exchanged magnets and I was holding yours and you were holding mine, but your walls were so thick they couldn't feel each other until then. But still, you can hold Vincent in your heart, that's your choice to make, isn't it?"

"It is," I agree. It is my choice to make, and the choice I will make. In fact, I've made that choice before she finished speaking, and there he is, I can feel him in that place where by our very nature we can only hold truth and love.

Yes. And. Honoring his innate right to choose and honoring my truth as well. Is this, I wonder, the true root of compassion? To hold in our heart even what we cannot hold in our life? I should write that in my red book, I think, or ask Rose to write it. I wonder if her handwriting will look like mine. I suspect she will have her own hand, her own signature, just as she has her own soul.

But then I see a line in the book, although I couldn't say if in my mind's eye it is written in my hand, hers, or if the script is in the printer's ink.

"Compassion does not condone. Neither does it condemn. It simply shows us the other through the eyes of truth and love."

There it is. Another path carved between the this or that, right or left, good or bad, pavements. Not yes/and but no/neither. Not approval, not punishment, just whatever is true and chosen from love.

That leads to the light I choose to follow. There may not be a path, but there is a way. And that is the way I will choose, no matter how many times I get lost, or hurt, or confused. No matter how much I doubt myself, or others, or even the divine. I will always know to come back to that path, because I will always be able to see the light at the end of it.

I've been looking at the soda can, watching the drops of water build on the leaf just above it until they're too ripe with water to cling to the leaf and fall, landing just where the red swirl of the can's logo reaches an apex, then redistributing themselves into smaller fragments as the tiny sound reaches my ears.

I raise my face to gaze into my sister's smile, seeing the love and in it that piece of me she's held in her heart. "That's us," I say. "That's all of us. Oceans and rivers and rain drops, but even as we go through all the shapes that water can take, we are never separate and yet always ourselves. Even ice will melt, and mist condense, the waters of the world are always coming back together and dividing again."

"Same," she agrees. "The same. We change shape, we come together, we divide, we come together." Nodding, she stands, stepping over a little rivulet that's formed on the ground that was too hard and dry to absorb it as quickly as it accumulated. Even water that's hiding in the soil and the plants and our bodies, I realize, will still change shape and return to its source someday.

I stand and follow her, stepping over the same tiny stream, picturing the pool in the grotto below and the ducks, surely joyful for the wetter world, and the roses taking the water into their roots and canes and holding drops like gems on their petals and leaves.

I turn my face to the sky, now showing brilliant blue and promising a steam bath once the sun is high. But there's water there too, in other forms. I feel the abundance of it, the world's waters. Like love. Not always where we want it to be, or in the shape we want it to take. Not always perceivable to our limited understanding. But there. And we are always part of it whether we believe it or not.

I'm not going to get much of a walk today. But I have traveled immeasurable distances. And it is enough.

SEPTEMBER

Organ music swells around me. The hymn tickles my memory, but the words won't come. Funerals were once a regular occurrence, these hymns once part of the fabric of my life. Thankfully, it has been years since I attended one.

The last note of the almost-familiar hymn thins and vibrates into quietude. The pause fills with a faint shuffling of feet, a sniffle, a cough, muffled whispers quickly stilled. Those muted sounds are all that I hear, but the very air suggests that the room behind me is filling to capacity. There are a few open spaces on the bench where I'm seated; I expect that people will come looking for them soon.

The organist has selected another hymn, this one I recognize as *In the Garden*. I sang that at my grandmother's funeral over twenty years ago. My last public performance, although I had not thought of it as such until now. By the time my father died, two and a half years later, I had already begun to lose my range. Within the next two years, I had given up ever singing again.

I try not to think of the casket in front of us. Rituals of death disturb me far more than death itself. Viewing the physical remains of some bright, loved soul has never given me comfort or closure. I want to honor the life, not gaze at a lifeless shape that was used and is no longer needed.

I'm taken back abruptly to my father's death bed. He'd been struggling to breathe for days. Home health nurses had come with a breathing machine. It helped to get air past the tumor in his throat, but nothing could stop it from growing. He could no longer swallow even the pudding I made, always one of his favorite foods. He sipped at water, forcing it down his throat with visible effort. His mind, having remained sharp through racking pain and numbing drugs that didn't numb enough, was now fuzzy from lack of oxygen.

I'd been with him night and day. My mother, my aunt, Tom, and I had become a hospital staff. We divided cooking, cleaning and nursing duties. We cared for the stream of guests who came to see our only patient. My aunt had my old bedroom. Tom and I slept on a pallet laid on the concrete floor of the laundry room. I woke frequently to stumble to my father's bedroom, sometimes because someone called me to come, sometimes because my inner voice sent me.

I watched the cancer consume his body, somehow revealing the spirit within. I hear again what I'd said to Glenn, "I never got to see the real person behind my father's face until he accepted that he was dying."

That last day, aching from days and nights that had no separation, I finally decided I had to have a shower. My soul needed renewing and my hair needed washing. Hot water would be the fastest remedy.

Aunt Pearl's voice from outside the shower stall, "You might want to come. I think he's going." I didn't take time to rinse the shampoo from my hair. I turned off the water, wrapped my soapy hair in a towel and threw on a robe. At my father's side, I watched the rise and fall of his ribs, the movement of his eyes behind the closed lids. They flickered open. I think he knew me.

I have no idea what went through my mind then. Now, with the funeral home's bench hard against my legs and back through the thin cushions, I try to remember. Was my memory true, or did I just need to believe I had been able to offer him the comfort of my presence? Had he really looked at me? Had he known that I was there? Did he feel the love that surrounded him?

I honestly don't know, this memory is too veiled to be trusted. Maybe he had never opened his eyes. Maybe he had looked at me, too near to leaving the physical world to remember our relationship in it. The organ is coming to the end of the chorus. The melody feeds me the words. "And the joy we share, as we tarry there, none other has ever known."

There is truth painted clear in the throb of the last organ note. For each of us at the bedside in that moment, the relationship of soul to soul was unique. He knew. His body may have been failing, his mind finally succumbing to the lack of oxygen. But his spirit felt the love and knew the unique stamp of each of us. Whatever the physical fact may have been I know that he felt the love around him, and recognized the source.

His breathing had eased then. Still shallow, but regular. The imminence of death had moved off a bit. I went back to the shower, turned the taps to hot and stepped inside. I remember the steam, hot water sluicing the tears from my eyes as fast as I produced them. The last of the shampoo rinsed, conditioner applied and rinsed, I stepped from the shower and reached for a towel.

My aunt's voice again, "Dixie, he's gone."

Guilt and sorrow overtake me again, just as they had then. I wasn't there. I was acutely aware of the irony. In our household, showers were for removing dirt. But I'd apparently been born with the idea that hot water, applied liberally and at length, was the cure for anything. How many times had I been scolded for taking too many showers? For staying in the shower too long?

Fitting then, that my taking time to indulge in a shower was the reason I was not there for him in that final moment. Guilt-frozen, dripping water onto the rug, steam rising off my skin, reflexively reaching for a towel, not noticing it was still soaked and soapy from being wrapped around my head just minutes ago.

I'd cried the last of my tears in that shower. I wouldn't cry again until the graveside service, going through the ritual of the funeral without a tear. In hindsight, I wonder if those who suspected more of our relationship than they let themselves acknowledge, thought my dry eyes reflected a relief on my part that he was gone. No one commented.

I told myself there was no cause for tears. I could hear his voice, the old voice in my head; "Stop that crying or I'll give you something to cry about." He had. He died. But even saying that to myself I knew it wasn't true. His soul was not in that body. My father was not dead. No cause for tears.

I'd never managed to cry when it would serve me, never managed to remain composed when that would serve me better. I had not given him my tears when he needed to see me yielding, I cried uncontrollably over animals lying dead in the road. Now, for once, I would be practical, I would be disciplined. I would not cry.

Which does not explain why, when the mortician and his assistant came to take his body, I felt called to witness what they did there. No one else moved to accompany them into the bedroom where he had spent the last of his days. No one stopped me or commented when I did.

They removed the bedclothes. I didn't expect them to strip the body, but they did. The young assistant was familiar. A younger brother of one of my classmates. His name comes back to me. It was Eric.

The physical casing that had been my father was laid, naked and lifeless, on the bed. They went about their business. I didn't blink, didn't cry.

I don't remember the first funeral I attended, a babe in arms. Born to older parents, raised in a religious community that honored death more dogmatically than life, funerals were routine. I had seen body after body, laid out in caskets. I had seen the remains of the old and the young. An aunt who wasn't my aunt by blood, but an icon in my life, white haired and peaceful in death as she had been in life. Grandparents, my father's father still an enigma, but both his first wife and his second wife dear to me, leaving me richer in experience for their living. A teenaged beauty queen I'd never known in life, looking like Sleeping Beauty with her blonde hair and painted rosy cheeks. My dearest Uncle James, who had taken me to the zoo every birthday for all of my life, his long body that he had once scrunched into the tiny seat of the choo-choo train now laid full length in the casket.

And never, *never* did I find peace in seeing them laid out "at rest." Why I had felt compelled to follow the men whose job it was to deal with the remains of life, I do not know. But I was, and I went.

My fists are clenched, tears streaming unheeded. Am I crying for Glenn, for my father, for me? What is the cause for tears?

The services are beginning, the rustling in the back stilled. The open spaces to either side of me on the bench are still open. Perhaps no one, slipping in late, wants to come so far to the front of the room. I'm trying to be unobtrusive about sopping up the tears. No tissue, since I never succumb to tears in public I hadn't come prepared. I'm just reaching for my purse to see if perhaps I have a forgotten tissue, even a paper napkin, when I feel a hand on my shoulder.

Ah, David is here after all. His long frame is dressed in slacks, button down shirt and dapper suit jacket. But an air of sunshine and freshly turned soil clings to him still. He squeezes my shoulder and reaches into a pocket, hands me a big, soft handkerchief. I take it, grateful, and start to slide over to make room beside me on the bench when I realize he is not alone. Red dress pressed for the occasion, Rose slips from behind him, slides easily past my knees and sits straight and calm on the bench. There is barely room for David on my other side, next to the aisle. He folds himself into the space and crosses his arms over his chest.

I'm struck by how much lighter I feel, having them present. How comforting it is to have their warmth tangibly overlapping my own. A small hand slips inside my elbow to grasp my hand where it lies in my lap. Her body tucked close, she leans against me and with her other hand pats my forearm.

Just so, do I remember adults comforting each other, death after death. The handshake, the other hand laid on the forearm to wordlessly express what no words could encompass. In a community that wasn't given to hugging, this restrained gesture still said it all.

What had she said to me? "Life is eternal. Love is eternal. It is only the frail physical body that cannot last forever." True, but Glenn's "frail physical body" was a representation of what we have come to love. Even this sister I never had has chosen to express herself as having a physical body. Her slim fingers against my arm ground me in a way that nothing else could. David's steady, even breath, my shoulder pressed tight against his side, provides a physical haven that I could not reach until he was sitting here with me.

Soul we may be, divine and eternal. But we manifest though a human body. That body, that physical presence, is a part of our truth as surely as any higher awareness might be. It is through that body that we act out our ideas, our thoughts, our inspirations. It is through a body that we share ourselves with others.

We connect, we communicate, we converge, by having a physical expression of our spirit. This comes to me not in words, but in one word. Communion. Sharing, mutuality, a transfer of one to another. Even in my past understanding of the word, watching the communion plate as it circulated amongst the faithful in the Sunday fellowship meetings, it represented a blending of body and spirit, person to person, becoming one.

Sea and shore, creating an illusion of separation, in order to rediscover their intimate truth. They are, always and forever, one.

I feel a physical and spiritual communion with Rose, my sister self, who was never born, and perhaps cannot die even in the physical sense. And with my climbing rose of a friend, whose mind I cannot fathom, but whose spirit speaks to me of home. Now I feel that sense spiraling to embrace every spirit in this room, sharing as we are, a common sense of loss that Glenn's physical being will not be seen in our world again.

Spiraling further, now enfolding every person who has ever felt loss. Everyone who has ever gone to bed with a stone where their heart was, trying not to let it shatter. Everyone who has ever woken to find their heart has turned to flesh once more, sorrow coming in again with the certainty of a tide, and who has found that it will go out, just as surely, making room for joy again.

The dance is danced, intimacy becomes communion, we become what we are. One.

The pastor's voice rises and falls, a backdrop only. The small hand on my arm, the solid warmth of a shoulder tight against my own, provide anchors in the swell of this new understanding of truth.

Experiencing the physical expression of the soul *is* a part of our spiritual journey. The death of the human "self" *is* a loss to those left behind. Like the applause after the last curtain, grief *is* right, it is homage to a life lived, a part played, a purpose fulfilled.

Even when we know there is no death, no one is ever "lost" to us, winter is only a time of rest, and the rose lives and will bloom again – this sense of loss, this longing to see and hear and *touch* is still part of the human experience we have chosen. To explore the gifts of being human, we allow ourselves to experience loss.

Heartbreak is nothing but a kind of growing pain. Like any growth spurt, it causes discomfort, but it results in new strength. Allowing your heart to break can be the beginning of knowing yourself to be whole.

There is a cause for tears. They are a part of the dance.

I hear music, but the organ is silent. Heartsong. Strong and pure, a collective thread of music coming to my inner ear from every soul that has reached this same understanding.

Hearts break so that they can grow bigger. Hearts break so that they can grow stronger. Hearts break so that they can grow more tender, more pliant, more able to stretch. Hearts break so that they can heal, and in healing, share that power with others.

Nothing can break our hearts unless there is first love. And if there is love, nothing can forever break our hearts.

I can see the words on my closed lids. Just the way they are printed in my little red book. How many times have I read them without understanding? And the entry on the opposite page. I had scoffed at it then, but today I know it for truth.

Time heals nothing. Time simply passes by. Love, given Time, heals all.

Communion – the sharing of body and spirit in love. Today I knew my first communion.

"His name was Ricardo, and he said he was a dancer." I begin my story as I've begun so many, sitting cross legged in the grass, a riot of roses at my back. In front of me, arms stretched wide and legs stretched long, David's presence takes up the bench and several feet around it. He's like a cat that way, he stretches outside of his physical space when he's at ease.

Rose is part of the riot of roses, sitting back to back with me, mirror images, her head tilted to rest between my shoulder blades. I don't know if she's listening, daydreaming, or sleeping, but it's good to feel the weight of her slim body resting against mine.

I describe the beautiful young man, his light-filled eyes and long, tapered fingers. How I'd noticed him as he greeted the flight attendant in the front cabin as he came aboard, and my sureness that he would choose the seat next to me.

"I don't know how I knew, or why it mattered. What are the odds, you know? Here I am in the window seat, with some average-as-church-on-Sunday-and-football-on-Monday guy in the aisle seat. They've announced that it's a full flight, just pick a seat and sit in it. And I watch this kid get on the plane and I just know we're going to have a conversation. There were probably ten or twelve people in front of him, but none of them took that seat."

As so often happens when I'm telling David a story, I'm transported in memory back to when *then* was *now*. I hadn't even looked up when the young man slid into the middle seat and put his backpack under the seat in front of him.

My little red book was open on my lap. I had thought I might read, maybe write in my journal. It had been such a crazy busy trip I'd hardly had time to write up my client notes, I hadn't written in my journal the whole time I'd been gone.

But the crazy busy trip had also left me crazy tired, I was dozing before we reached altitude. I woke up, startled to find dark eyes, almond shaped and decorated with fringed lashes, looking intently at my face.

He'd looked away, down at the book lying open on my lap. Then he looked back at me. "I'm sorry. I read it."

Looking at the entries on the pages that are showing, I'd seen:

Having passion is not difficult and costs nothing. Following your passion will present challenges and comes with a price. But can you calculate the price of not pursing your passion?

And on the other side of the page:

The saddest form of self-limitation is the editing of self-expression. When you limit self-expression you limit understanding of self. For how can you know yourself if you cannot see your self expressed?

I'd looked back at his face, found him meeting my gaze. "I like that," he says bluntly, pointing at the pages. "It's true."

"I think it was the way he said, 'It's true,' that really grabbed me." David's eyes are closed, listening to the story, but his eyebrows twitch upwards at that. He understands.

"All he said then was, 'I dance.' He's fond of sentences with only two or three words, I guess. Then he added, 'That's how I know. It's true. If I couldn't dance, or create dance, I wouldn't know who I am.' And then he just told me his life story."

I go on to describe the truth I'd heard between the lines of what the boy had actually said. The sense of being something other than human, super-powered, moving like fire, like water, freezing into sudden stillness of stone while other dancers took up the story and danced out their part. The way the very air would go electric when he danced, so that he forgot his feet were landing on a wooden stage, but rather thought that he sprang into each leap from the cushiony grass of some primordial meadow.

His words plodded, but his voice was liquid with longing, his hands and face told me what he wanted to say. So I tell it to David the way I heard it; it makes a truer story.

"His name," I say again to David and to the maybe-listening Rose, "was Ricardo. I suppose that's the Spanish version of Richard, isn't it?" I don't hear his reply, because I'm hearing a husky voice telling me "Dixie is the feminine diminutive for Richard, so it means the same."

"He's the oldest of nine, his parents never went to college. He's determined to set the bar high for his little brothers and sisters. He wants to dance, maybe even teach, but his *real* passion is choreography. Of everything he told me, I could tell he was most proud of the dance he wrote in honor of his sister who died young."

On I go, David listening with his eyes on my face or on his roses, I can never tell. He gives a quiet hum of understanding when I tell him about the boy's sister, dead before she began living, and another hum of disdain when I tell him about Ricardo's search for a religion he could accept.

"David, it is a horrible dilemma for him. His mother is an atheist. Hard core. She believes we are no more than evolved animals. If he accepts that truth, his sister was only animated elements, and when her body died, there was nothing left of her but memory.

"His mother is also a lesbian. So if he accepts the *church's* truth that his sister's spirit is eternal, then he also accepts that his mother is doomed to burn in hell for her choice of a sexual partner. He needed a different story."

"And did you give him one?" David challenges me, and I feel Rose leaning against me, listening for my reply. "Did you give him a different story?"

I sit with that, eyes closed in memory, drinking in the heat of the sun and the scent of the roses. I think I will always smell that perfume when I turn my gaze inward in search of answers.

"I gave him *my* story," I answer finally. "Actually, I gave him my truth."

David nods. After a couple of seconds or lifetimes he echoes me, "Your truth? What is your truth, Dixie? Have you discovered it yet?"

The universe condenses to just us three, us and the roses. As so often happens when I sit here with David, the traffic and the birds are silent, no jogger's footsteps sounding from the path just ten feet off. Everything is removed from my knowing except David's question, his intense patience, and the perfume of the roses guiding me inward.

"We *can* deny our soul if we choose, there must be something to be learned from that. But once we *acknowledge* that we are soul, that our body is just a form that we've chosen in order to be a part of this human experience, it all comes down to the same thing. We are here to have experiences that a soul cannot have, do things a soul cannot do, without taking on the illusion of limitations, without pretending to be confined in a body and bound by the laws of a physical universe.

"It doesn't matter, does it, if we believe we were put here by a divine power that is separate from ourselves, if we believe we're on a karma wheel of life and reincarnation, or if we believe we are a part of the divine universal source. It still comes down to the same thing."

David has pulled in his arms and legs – he's coiled and waiting. He leans forward on his bench, eyes intent on mine. "What is that thing, Dixie? That thing it all comes down to?"

Rose has slipped around to sit facing me; two sets of eyes watch my face for the truth in my response. "Whether we believe we come here by choice, we're fated here by karma, or we're put here by God, we are *here* to do the one thing we can*not* do as pure spirit – experience ourselves as separate.

"We have experiences, and those experiences change us, they change others. We enrich the tapestry of reality by changing the reflection. What we *do* here is not real, but the changes that we create *through* what we do here, that is real.

"We are already infinite, we cannot grow. But we expand into the *awareness* of our infinite natures by pretending limitations and loving enough to break through them.

"We choose this existence to experience new ways of loving, new ways of seeing, new ways of being. Through experience we create gifts, we unwrap them. Through love, we share them. With each gift, we move a little deeper into the infinite ocean that is our *true* home."

A buzz of power as physical as an electrical current is running through my veins, my blood hums with it, my heart sings with it, and my mind spreads from horizon to horizon just to try to take it in.

"That's *it*, isn't it David?" Now I am challenging *him*. "We are here to experience. To have experiences and share experiences. But the story is never about what happened, that's not the truth of the soul's experience, it's always about how we changed because of what happened. How we used the experience to take us closer to our divine self. How we tell the story of the experience in a way that takes us back to love, and to the truth of being one."

I watch his face for validation, but what I see is surprise. His eyebrows have climbed nearly to his hairline and his mouth is slightly open. "How we tell the story of the experience in a way that takes us back to love," he repeats, but it isn't a confirmation, he's tasting it to see if it feels right on his tongue. I look from his face to the face of the girl sitting at his feet. Her eyebrows are raised as well, but she looks more smug than surprised.

"Yes. It is." *He* may not be sure, but suddenly I am. That buzz of power wouldn't be thrumming through my body if I weren't telling it true.

"So many people experience the same event, or similar but separate events, but their *story* is not the same. The gifts they find, and hopefully unwrap and share, those gifts are in the way *they* choose to tell the story, not in the actual events. The gifts are not in what *happened* to them, but in how they interpret what happened. We choose our interpretation, we choose our gifts. We *choose* our truth."

I'm up on my knees, not remembering how I got there, leaning forward, wanting to touch him, wanting to see if this current can leap between us. Words are so powerful and such a poor method of communicating.

Then I understand that too. "That's why we create language, even though it's limited. Imagine if we *could* mind link. I wouldn't *tell* you my stories, I'd just open my mind to you, and you would see it exactly as I did. You'd see the gifts *I* need from my story, but not the gifts *you* need. I wish I could because I want you to understand me. But it is a greater thing for me to open a pathway for *you* to understand *you*. You won't do that through *my* interpretation of my story, but the limitation of language leaves room for you to interpret it for yourself and take away the gifts *you* need from *my* experience."

"It's all story," I say softly again. The current is passing, leaving me washed clean, transparent. "Music, pictures, words, dance even … all story, all an offering of gifts. We have experiences so we can receive gifts. We share the story of our experiences so we can share gifts. It's true, isn't it?" I look from him to Rose and back again. "The whole "human" experience, David, it's just one big gift exchange!"

He throws himself against the back of the bench, helpless with the release that only laughter brings. It takes me back to the first time we met, him laughing like this at my asking what kind of rose he would be.

He recovers gradually, finally leaning forward to fix me in that penetrating gaze again. "Tell me the rest of the story," he demands. "And tell it true."

I have to retrace my mental footsteps to realize he wants to hear more about Ricardo. "He's a storyteller too," I say when I have found the thread again. "The dance he choreographed in memory of his sister? He called it *The Muse and the Mage.*"

I paint for them the premise of the dance; the girl, despairing that she had no talent of her own, invited to become a powerful muse. The only caveat being that she must give up her earthly life.

Transformed through magic and dance into a flitting spirit in a white gauzy gown, she inspires artist after artist to greatness, pulling images, words and music from them like cotton candy spun from a wheel.

My voice goes on, but my eyes aren't seeing them anymore. Rose's red dress, the bench, David's long frame on it, all gone.

The mage. I word-paint the mage. Magician and sage in one, the most powerful of magic workers, come into power on his inaccessible mountaintop all alone. He's never had a master, he's coaxed or forced his wisdom and knowledge from everything around him. He's stolen it from the wind and the trees, from the animals and the earth, from rumors born on the air. He comes onto the stage bound, tendrils of magic that he cannot see hold him fast, even as they lend him power.

I tell them how the mage stirs and pulls at his bindings, weary of his mastery, longing for something new to learn, some path to power he has yet to discover. In his restless search his casting mind snags at the little muse – drawing her, like a lodestone calls the compass point, to his high aerie.

But the muse reminds him that all paths to power begin *within*. He has yet to plumb the depths of himself, has yet to express all the beauty and wisdom he was *born* with because he has been so intent on possessing the beauty and wisdom he sees in the world outside.

As the muse dances out her plea for him to look inside, to find the magic in his own beautiful spirit, the magic that is his and his alone, stolen from no one and nothing, the mage becomes still. The bindings unravel, the muse takes one end in her little hand and, dancing joyfully around the now radiant mage, she unwinds the tangled bindings, letting them fall to the ground where they become streams of water feeding a great river that can be heard through the music. All that magic becoming one with the greater magic, indivisible and indistinguishable, but still its unique self.

I tell it better than Ricardo, how could I not? He told the story through descriptions of costume and motion, but I have been practicing telling mine in words. Now I tell *his* story, the story he created to honor the life of his sister, as eloquently as I know how.

I suck in a deep breath, the first full breath I've taken in many seconds. "Finally I ask him if he's sure that the muse did not, in the end, find her own pathway to power and become a mage herself." I laugh, remembering the astonishment on Ricardo's face at my question.

"I wonder how long it will be before the rest of the world gets to see that danced out, the little muse ending the last scene by donning a mage's robe over her white gauze gown."

David's smile is a mischievous ray of sunshine after a summer thunderstorm. He nods contemplatively, "I'm wondering when I'll get to see that, myself."

I ponder, that night, sitting on the starlit patio, the scent of my own roses heavy in the air, what David meant. Did he see the little muse in Rose, had he noticed that she was beginning to write her own story, create her own alchemy?

Or was he referring to me? And where did he fit in? The mage? I could see that, if his magic was what made the roses bloom. What role did each of us play in the story he was telling himself?

"Does it matter?" I hear her in my mind and open my eyes to find her sitting cross legged at my feet, my little red book in her hands.

"Does it matter?" she repeats. "Your story isn't his to write. He'll write his own. And now, I'm writing mine. But you need never surrender your power again. *You* will write your own story."

With a smile, she opens the book in her hands and holds it up to me like an offering. I take it, noting that it is opened to the center pages, one short phrase per page, just like the others. On one side I read;

There is nothing you can not, because there is nothing that you are not. To become all that you can be, you must only accept all that you are.

And on the other, the simple phrase that had changed my life thirty years ago, had *saved* my life thirty years ago:

You can let someone else tell your story. But why? It is your story, the power is yours to make of it anything you choose. Why throw all that power away?

Yes, there is my truth, in the heart of this little book, hidden until I was ready to believe in it again. A reminder of power. Of truth.

My story. My truth. My choice. To accept all that I am, to be all that I can, and to write my own story so that it is true and meaningful. To me.

I close the book and hand it back to her.

"I think I'll make it a love story," I say, offering no other explanation.

Because we are one, she understands.

OCTOBER

Sunset on the Kansas prairie. We walk slowly toward the walls of stone. Rose keeps pace with me, my little sister self, her slender arm tight around my waist, snuggled close under the arm I have around her shoulder.

The wind is settling as the sun sinks, touching my sun-warmed skin with a chill that speaks of autumn. Not yet the biting wind of the winter wolf, but nipping, the wolf pup at play. In another month the skies will turn cornflower blue, and the leaves will be a riot of burnished metals; gold and bronze and copper blazing on every horizon. Now the trees are still rose-blush and crimson, and the sky is a haze of sunset color; dust from the fields forming a scrim of captured light in pink and orange and purple. I feel my heart break a little to let it in, and my arm tightens around my sister's shoulders.

She smiles up at me, an easy, wordless acknowledgment of shared wonder. Our steps stop in unison, and we stand, leaning into each other, facing the glory in the west, hearing the birds calling their "day is ended" song. I feel the tingle of power rippling between us, the impossible, unavoidable, miracle of being.

In the ripples of power, she is the older, wiser self and I am the carefree toddler. I am the mother and she the crying child. I am fallen, wounded, she the warrior riding to my rescue. All the possibilities ripple out in simultaneous choices of being, as real as we are real and as fleeting as the forms we wear. Every story true, if it takes us where we choose to go.

I close my eyes and see on my eyelids the afterimage of the burning sun. Against that brilliance is written the dedication in my little red book, "For you who have been, who are, and who will be – we are one."

And on the cover, beneath the careful stitching, the tiny pricks of a needle's passing, carrying threads since removed. The pattern I have never been able to recognize. A rose.

Tears creep from under my eyelids. I let them. All those years of refusing to cry, now the faucets open at the lightest touch. We turn as one to move into the shelter of the castle wall, lean against the stone, and let our skin breathe in the warmth the sun has left behind.

We are one.

Yes we are. We are complete alone or together because we experience apart and separate only so that we can find our way back to the truth of being one.

I am not surprised to hear a whuffle and to open my eyes to see the big nose almost touching mine, to see the wise eye turned on me, or to see the ears twitch forward and back, listening for the silent heart call that brought her mount here from whatever possibility he had been inhabiting.

She is going. It is time. I feel it too, a loop coming back to its place of origin, a season drawing to a close. Of course she will leave the way she came, a slim straight figure in a rose-red dress, perched on the bare back of this magnificent horse.

His breath stirs my hair, and he catches a few strands between his lips. He ducks and tosses his head a bit to pull on my hair, a gentle tease. Then he angles himself to present his near side to us, ready for her to mount up and ride. Without a glance at me, she vaults easily to his back.

I'm stung. She is leaving without even a hug goodbye. It's fine and well to know she won't really be gone, even to admit that she may never have been, but I still want the story to end with an embrace that says all that we are to each other.

To my surprise she doesn't take up the reins and move the big horse off. She slides high over his withers and reaches down a hand to me. My eyebrows go up of their own volition. She gives me a lopsided grin and a wink, her arm still stretched toward me.

Okay then. I step onto an outcropping of wall and reach for her hand. The stallion sidles closer and stands stock still while I mount, not so gracefully as she, but sliding on smoothly enough. I wrap one arm around her waist, reach past her to take a handful of mane in my other hand. Looking at the ground in front of us I see a single shadow. Me, the horse, and my sister, the last rays of the sun behind us, cast a shadow that cannot be recognized as horse or human.

The language of one soul reaching out to another, that is the language of truest love. A love that does not seek to possess or persuade, to conquer or submit, but only to speak and be understood. That language shows the true shape of us, all else is but shadow and reflection.

"All else is but shadow," I think, looking at the blob that we cast on the ground. No wonder I had not understood the words in my little book. I needed this moment to know my true shape.

Tightening my thighs and knees against the smooth sides of the stallion and taking a firmer grip on his mane, I lean into her. "Go," I whisper.

I barely hear the "tsk" of her tongue moving against her teeth, but we are suddenly wheeled about and moving smoothly toward the horizon, following the same path I'd watched them take the first day I'd seen horse and rider on the open prairie. I glance over my shoulder at the parapet walls. Is that a solitary figure squinting against the sun to watch us ride away?

"It will be well," I send a thought back to the silent watcher. "This love story has the best kind of ending, no ending at all."

Then I turn myself to listen to the sun setting, the magical heart song of grasses rushing, hooves beating, birds warbling and woven into it all, the distinct smell of roses.

NOVEMBER

"This will be my last Thanksgiving in this house."

Alice unclenches her hands and lays them palm up in front of her on the kitchen table.

I choke on a memory. Thanksgiving in my childhood home, over twenty years ago. My father, frail, tired even by the effort of using his walker to move from one room to another, the cancer gnawing at his bones, but no bitterness in his voice, saying, "This will be my last Thanksgiving."

Then, I had said, "Dad, you can't know that." But he knew more than I.

Now, I hear the truth in her words. I have no response but to slip my hand into her open palm.

She covers it with her other hand, layers of flesh and bone, life lines and love lines, calluses and fingerprints.

We sit.

My mind wanders forward and back, mingling scenes from that Thanksgiving years ago with the imagined upcoming holiday in this house that has enfolded me in its rooms the way a family embraces a long lost child.

We'd been next to the piano, my father and I, when he said those words. I can still see the keys — ivory and ebony framing his straight back as he sank gingerly onto the piano bench. As if, having told me what to expect, he could allow himself the weakness of needing to sit.

The piano had been his gift to me. A mind-bending, heart-opening, surprise gift.

From the time I could remember, he'd been dead set against my learning to play an instrument. Associations of his father and sisters playing in depression era dance bands? The remembered sting of being one of the non-musical members of his family and forever barred from the harmony of their voices and instruments? I never really understood his reluctance to have me explore my musical tendencies—but, until the day he took an unexpected turn into Hille's Music Store, I never knew that he liked to hear me play and sing.

It was my grandmother, the fiery matriarch of his family, who first decided I should have lessons. In love with music, singing since I was old enough to learn the words, I'd been picking out songs on a little electric organ. A child's toy, really. Grandma thought I might have a gift.

She loved classical music. Although she had played along with my grandfather's banjo and their daughter's fiddles and guitars, she spoke with disdain of the folk tunes and ballads I preferred. I should learn to play *real* music, she decreed, and she was going to see to it I had the chance.

She located an old upright in someone's garage. She bought it and had it delivered and tuned. And she gave my father a check for my lessons. I was ten.

At ten, I thought my grandmother was rich. She lived in California and took fabulous trips. She came to visit once or twice a year, sharing my little room. During the day, she wore big wheels of glittering jewels clipped to her earlobes and big rings of mother of pearl on her fingers. At night, she wore bright, flowing gowns she called muumuus and told me tales of islands where the sands were gold, the people were brown, and pigs were cooked whole in pits on the beach. Her life was exotic and impossible and intoxicating to a girl who woke up summer mornings to oatmeal and birdsong and a garden that needed weeding.

Even my father was in awe of her. She was the only person he obeyed. Without question. He might squirm, and he might have harsh words to say later. But he never said them to her. And when she told him what do to, he did it.

So when she bought the piano, handed him a check, and told him to make sure I got lessons, I knew I was about to learn to play the piano. Learn to play it right, from notes on a page, not making up what I heard in my head and picking it out on the keys.

Later, I realized that my grandmother wasn't rich. Not at all. She lived in a tiny apartment just blocks from Hollywood and Vine. She rode the bus, she shopped the sales, she watched her pennies so that she could take the tours with other "seniors" to places she'd dreamed of going when she was a young Kansas farm wife with seven kids in a depression economy.

But she counted her pennies well-spent to know that I would learn to play the music she loved.

So once each week I went from my fifth grade classroom to the home of Mrs. Thomas. She was a young mother, with long thin fingers that went from showing me how to arrange my little hands on the keyboard, to plucking her toddler's fingers off her jeans. I learned to play *Mary Had a Little Lamb* the way the music was written, thumb crossing under fingers instead of flopping uselessly while my fingers picked out the melody. My thumbs learned to rest next to each other on middle C, and my stubby little fingers learned to move in harmony as I played scales, up and down and down and up.

I learned that some keys played at the same time made no sense to the ears at all – while, when they were combined with other notes, produced rich layers of meaning and depths of innuendo that left colors in the air where they faded and died.

I learned that keys weren't only the bars of black and white that played notes when you touched them, keys also indicated when some notes were to be played as a different note. When an F wasn't really an F, but was an F sharp in disguise. I learned that by changing the key you changed the notes, and you changed the mood. Different keys, I discovered, told different stories.

When my grandmother returned the next summer, I had learned enough to be dangerous. Sometimes I think the gift of my piano was my father's reward for getting the best of his mother.

I didn't mean it as a trick. I just wasn't blessed with patience.

My mother used to remind me, "Dixie, patience is a virtue."

Once I'd become self-aware enough to know it for truth, I answered defiantly, "Maybe it is, but it isn't one of mine!"

However, I *was* given the virtue of imagination, and being impatient to play the music I could hear, but not yet read, I made it up.

I would sit at the old upright – stained black wood polished every week by my own hands, my siblings' graduation pictures, now more than ten years outdated, looking down at me.

My sister with perfect skin and gilded hair, pearls in her ears and around her throat, a vision I could never grow up to be. My brother in his military uniform, eyes already distant, jaw set in a firm line. Carefully avoiding looking at their faces, I would pick a key. I hadn't learned what they were called then, majors and minors weren't part of Mrs. Thomas' curriculum for first year students, but I'd pick a mood and a key that matched the story in my head and start to play.

I'd lose myself in it. My eyes would close, my foot working the sustain pedal and my fingers roaming the keyboard while my mind escaped to islands where the wash of the sea and cry of the gulls were the only sounds I heard. Or to mountains where the clouds pressed close against my cheeks, and the laughter of the gods at play was carried by the wind to my mortal ears.

In the notes, the chords, the ripples of liquid sound, I heard Demeter crying for her child and Psyche crying for her Cupid. I heard Queen Liliuokalani crying for her island country and the mermaids crying for their sister. I played laughter too, bubbling brooks and rivulets of it, sun streams of it, tall grass prairies of it, moon dances of it. In my fingers' flight across the keys, all of nature begged me to laugh when others cried, and believe in life's magic where others saw only tragic endings.

My grandmother, listening to the laughing and crying of the keys, said to my mother, "I don't recognize that piece? What is it?"

My mother, nearly crying from trying not to laugh, says she replied with a straight face, "You've probably never heard it, I think it's fairly new."

I'd never meant it as a trick, nor yet as a joke. I hadn't meant anything by it at all. The only meaning for me was in the keys of laughing and crying and dancing and flying. They never understood.

So I graduated to classes with a Mrs. Connelly, who waited for me in a little room at the top of the stairs above a shop downtown. Already settled into a wide, worn recliner next to the spinet piano, she waited until I was settled on the bench. Then she wound up the metronome and commanded me to play.

She never touched the keys, although she would reach to thump me when my wrists sagged, and my fingers went flat. Or when my elbows flew wide, or my toe tapped the count. Those things were "bad form."

But as I learned to read the music, I forgot how to play.

By the year of the surprise gift, I was only playing what I could read, but I still found joy in the keys. I turned more and more to sight reading what I could sing; old sheet music from the Tin Pan Alley days like *Fly Me to the Moon* and *Let Me Call You Sweetheart*, and my favorites, the sweet ballads from my mother's high school music class songbook, *The Golden Book of Favorite Songs*.

Here I found stories like *The Minstrel Boy* and *The Last Rose of Summer*, and my voice, trained to gospel style phrasings and harmonies by years of singing hymns, came into its own. It became my instrument of choice, and I played with vocal harmonies the way I had once played with scales and chords.

I learned later that those were the songs that earned me my father's indulgence of a brand new piano. My mother told me, years after he was gone, that he would sit at our kitchen table, where he could hear but not be seen, and listen while I sang the old songs that most of my generation had never heard.

It was the classic, *The Wildwood Flower*, that did it. My grandmother would have scoffed. It wasn't a challenging arrangement, but the melody requires range and power, and the story begs a sensitivity of tone that most singers cannot manage.

"She sounds just like Mother Maybelle," or that's what my mother told me he would say. High praise from my father. He'd given up listening to secular music after professing into their faith, but The Carter Family had been his favorite.

Of course, that winter's day, walking along the sidewalk in Independence, Kansas, one foot in front of the other with my eyes and mind locked onto the long windows full of instruments and music stands that fronted Hille's Music Store, I didn't know my father even listened when I made the music I loved.

He walked us into the annex that held the pianos, formal uprights and delicate spinets, curvaceous baby grands and even one full concert grand propped open to reveal its heart of strings and hammers.

"If we got you a piano," he began as I gaped in hungry wonder, "which one would you choose?"

I didn't dare to take him seriously, just as I didn't dare to put a finger on the gleaming keys of the grand. I shot him a look that must have plainly shown my hunger and my fear of being caught in foolish hope and belief. He just nodded.

I played some scales on one of the uprights, then on the spinets. I stroked the wood and opened the lids to watch the hammers tap the strings as my finger tapped the keys. A salesman came and spoke with my parents. I was aware of him only as a voice that didn't belong.

Finally I slid onto a bench of light wood, looked down at the run of keys below the Wurlitzer logo and played the first piece that came to memory; from sheet music given to me by my grandmother, *The Blackhawk Waltz*.

And fell in love.

I suppose it completed the cycle for my father to rest himself on that same bench and put the last year of his life in my hands.

May the circle be unbroken.

I remember that Thanksgiving, the house full of kids and grownups, warm from the fire in the wood stove and the overworked oven and the body heat of more people than those rooms had held in years. My nieces' little girls, each looking so much like their mothers had at that age that we agreed the clock had turned back twenty years. There had been a storm, and my brother and sister stayed to wait it out, so the talking went on into the night.

It was the only Thanksgiving I remember feeling like one big family, not divided into first family of my brother and sister, and second family of me. I ate dinner with the grownups, sitting next to Tom at the table, instead of sitting with the grandkids in the next room. If I had something to say, I was given space to say it, and no one scoffed at my notions. I was finally a peer, an initiated member of the clan.

This Thanksgiving, the one coming in just two weeks, I'd be sitting with kids and grownups both. No division at this dinner, Alice had decided. And Tom would be here with me; his family would have their dinner on Saturday following Thanksgiving, so we could do both. I wondered how he would take to the friends I'd made and how they would take to him. If nothing else, I knew he'd be a hero to the kids – he's the kind of guy kids instantly fall for and can't get enough of.

"What about the piano?" I ask Alice.

I've given her no context for the question, but she doesn't seem to need it. Perhaps she's been following along with my waking go-back dream. Her grip on my hand tightens for a moment, then releases as she pushes back her chair to stand.

"I'm leaving it." She smiles out at the herbs drooping in their beds, the roses valiantly showing a few brave blooms and optimistic buds.

"I've asked that they use some of the funds from the trust to bring in a music teacher. Someone who can teach the kids piano and voice or just lead sing-a-longs. And David will be back in the spring to tend to the roses and teach the kids how to treat growing things. Those are things that help the spirit blossom and I want them to have that.

"It won't be just living space, you know. The upstairs will be temporary housing for families in need of shelter, but the downstairs is going to be a haven for kids and adults of all ages and all backgrounds to come, and learn, and just *be*. I've been talking with the Board of Directors, and they've initiated alliances with a number of other organizations to create programs for kids and adults both. We'd like to have courses on business and entrepreneurship and," she took a breath and turned her eyes back to meet mine, "we'd like to involve you if you're willing."

My heart answers for me. It declares that I am more than willing. I nod, wordless. She understands.

"I'll visit," she reminds me. "I'm keeping a small suite of rooms on the second floor. It's a place where I can live when I am here, or where anyone who comes to learn our model, or be a guest teacher, can stay.

"I want to be near my parents now, but a piece of my heart will always be in this city, in this house, at this table." She rests her fingertips on the table like a seer on a crystal ball and smiles, the first full smile I've seen on her face since we buried Glenn. It reaches her eyes, and the sun is strengthened by it.

"Did I tell you what we're calling it? When the foundation takes it over?"

I shake my head.

"It will be the Rose Haven. Most people will think it's named for the roses, of course. And that's all right. But Rose is my middle name, and Glenn used to tease me that I couldn't be his "wild Irish rose" because I'm not Irish, nor his "yellow rose of Texas" because I'm not from Texas. So he called me his Blushing Rose because I used to blush so easily."

She's blushing now, and I can tell from the dimple that appears in one cheek that she knows I am following her thoughts.

"Come here, I want to teach you the song he used to sing for me." She takes my arm and guides me toward the conservatory where her old piano holds court.

I don't protest, even though she knows there is no reason for me to learn a song. My father's gift has a place of pride in my home, but I haven't played in many years, the sheet music is all lost, and my voice, vocal chords ravaged by years of sinus infections, will no more hold a note than it will shatter glass.

But I follow her willingly and sit beside her on the bench as she rests her fingers on the keys.

She plays a few bars, lightly humming until her voice is warmed.

"It's a hymn he learned in his church. When he was married to Beth Ann's mother they went to the United Universalist church, you know. After she left, he didn't go, but he treasured their music and I used to play and sing it with him. This one was his favorite."

Her voice is light and clear. I miss the first line or two just wanting to harmonize with her, feeling my throat stretch and yearn with notes I can no longer produce. But my subconscious mind has recorded what I've missed, and the words begin to sink in.

Come sing a song with me
Come sing a song with me
Come sing a song with me
That I might know your mind.

The last longing line of the simple verse soaks through me. Leaves me drenched in want. Yes, that is why I grieve that I cannot raise my voice with hers, because in sharing song and story we learn minds and hearts.

She has gone on to a chorus now;

And I'll bring you hope
When hope is hard to find
And I'll bring a song of love
And a rose in the winter time.

While I'm catching the breath that sticks in my throat at the simple, joyful offering made by her voice and the words, she's moved into the next verse.

Come walk in rain with me
Come walk in rain with me
Come walk in rain with me
That I might know your mind.

And then the chorus again, layers of simplicity ending with the impossible promise of a rose in the winter time.

The next two verses follow the same pattern,

Come dream a dream with me

And the final verse,

Come share a rose with me
Come share a rose with me
Come share a rose with me
That I might know your mind.

She repeats the chorus and lets the last note fade, her fingers lying still on the keys. She leans against me, shoulder to shoulder, and I tilt my head to the side so that our temples touch. I wonder if she can sense the spirit brush of a kiss on her forehead the way I sense it on mine. I haven't seen my sister since our ride across the prairie last month, but I know her touch and feel her presence often.

"Well," she lifts her head and takes her fingers off the keys. "I have work to do, and I could use your help if you have time. Glenn left a lot of small things that are to be sent to various people he has known through the years. I've gathered them up, and made a list of names and addresses, but they need to be boxed and mailed, and it's something I'd rather not have a stranger do. It will be so much easier with your company."

It doesn't require an answer. We move in unison into the dining room where the long table, which will soon hold a feast for our new family, is covered in memorabilia and trinkets, boxes, note cards, and tape.

Bits of Glenn's life, there on the table, include autographed pictures of celebrities he's met, baseballs he's caught or been given, commemorative medals and awards. Remnants of his *material* life, now gifts to be shared with others. How much richer are we who shared the gift of his soul?

As we box and tape, wrap and address, I think about gifts. A piano I no longer play, a huge old house half-empty for years, roses, now nestling down for a winter's rest in their sunny space. Come share a song, and hope, and roses.

And love.

I remember my answer to Alice when she asked me how we heal.

"We love. We love and we become whole."

I understand now that healing requires more than *feeling* love. It requires leaving behind the need, the want, and the fear, and choosing love instead. Choosing to *believe* in it, choosing to *allow* it, choosing to *hold* to it, choosing to *share* it. Even when that choice seems as unlikely as a rose in the wintertime, we choose.

We choose love.

It's the only story that makes any sense. The only truth that leads me where I want to go.

I choose love.

ACKNOWLEDGEMENTS

"Nothing is more powerful than an idea whose time has come."

Victor Hugo, French poet and novelist

It was February of 2012 when I sat in front of a cozy fire and finished reading this story aloud to the one person who knew why I'd written it. I watched tears making lines on his cheeks as he sat in silence for some time, and when at last we could talk I knew the story was not yet to be released into the world. Despite generous praise and encouragement from him and other early readers, I put it aside.

For more than a decade I have walked my own paths to be ready to share this story, unpacking and codifying the practices that brought me to this place of truth so that I could help others navigate their own stories and step into their own power to create the lives they choose to live. And I've waited for the time to be right in the world for the story to be told. The first I know is true. I am ready, and I've tested myself and my methods and proved that the concepts and principles in this story hold true and have the power to transform lives. The second is yet to be determined, but I believe that this idea of choosing love over everything else is an idea whose time has come, and that I am only one among many who are ready to share their stories of life, love, and wholeness.

The gratitude I feel for those who contributed to this story, who held space and witnessed the transformations required for this story to come to life, and who have waited patiently (or at least without yelling at me too much) for the story to be published, is beyond my ability to put into words and I cannot list them all in these pages. You know who you are, and how dearly you are loved.

I owe gratitude, also, to all the characters between these covers. Whether "real" or "imagined" you are all real to me and I love you and appreciate your gifts in my life.

There are a few specific people however, without whom this story would not have been brought to life in this way and in this time. These people have shared my path and my transformations, they have guided my work, and they have trusted me to guide them in their own discovery of power. Most recently and most directly, my editor, Maria Rodgers O'Rourke, whose delicate and nuanced touch molded the story into a more powerful transformational arc and whose experience with my methods helped to ensure that the story stayed true to my principles and teaching. Also, many thanks to the talented creator of the art you see on the cover, photographer and visual artist (as well as fellow coach) Carol Nichols, who turned my journey through the seasons into a magical work of art. Michael Beas and his team at Atlas Elite Publishing Partners not only made it their business to make this book successful, but also made it their mission to support me and stay true to the message of this story.

No idea or realization comes without inspiration from other creators. I've had the privilege to know and learn from many colleagues and teachers. In particular, Tom Ruwitch, storyteller and marketing maven, who has been my mastermind partner since before this book was even an idea and whose solid support and uncanny insights into who I am and what I bring to the world gave me clarity and courage when I seriously considered burning the manuscript, wiping the hard drives, and pretending this book had never been written. Christopher Duncan, whose unique amalgamation of ancient truths and modern science in the Magnetic Mind Method gave me structure for the work I had been doing by intuition and instinct and elevated my abilities to transform energy and experience. Robert Fritz, whose brilliant teachings on how structure and identity create our reality was a lifesaver during my years as a business consultant and have continued to inform and reform my understanding of myself and the human dynamic. And of course, Richard Bach, whose book *Illusions: The Adventures of a Reluctant Messiah* ignited and illuminated so many truths when I was 14 and whose wit, wisdom, and wonder continued to inspire my own discoveries so many years later.

My deepest gratitude goes to family, of blood and of choice. To my Sister-of-blood, I have so much respect for the way you have navigated your own truths and so much love for you and what you bring to the world. To my Sister-of-spirit, Rose you have been in my heart from the beginning of my self and you will always be a part of who I am. And to all the sisters and brothers who have endured their own experiences of abuse and who are navigating their own truths and choices, I honor your journey and hope you always find the power to choose love.

Finally, I give love and homage to the men who are intrinsically woven into this story and my life. My father, who only learned to choose love when he was losing everything else but who chose it so simply and completely that I could never doubt it again. Tom Gillaspie, who may no longer be my spouse but who will always be a part of the story. Philip Penrose, in whom I have met my match, my mate, my love, and my choice for co-creating the rest of my life. And the one I called my dragon, who was also my friend, who always asked after this book the way you might ask after a family member and to whom I can now say … "It is complete."

About the Author

Dixie Gillaspie is the author of *Just Blow It Up – Firepower for Living an Unlimited Life*, an instruction manual for Super Creators who are ready to blast through barriers and create anything they choose. In her 30 years of consulting and coaching business leaders, thought leaders, and entrepreneurs she's celebrated the cultural shifts toward bringing soul awareness and understanding into business creation and she's learned to love her natural tendency to navigate life with one foot in the world of spirit and the other planted on terra firma.

Since early childhood Dixie has been addicted to story and allergic to "can't" and her stories and poems, like her work with clients, are always about the journey from limited to limitless, powerless victim to powerful creator, and impossible dream to current reality. Dixie lives in St. Louis, MO with two dogs, two cats, and her partner-in-all-things, Philip.

RESOURCES

For group discussion or deeper contemplation and uncovering of your own truths the author periodically adds resources to her website at DixieGillaspie.com.

Resources available at the time of publication include:

- Book Club Discussion Guide
- Study Group Guide
- I AM Activation Meditation

Scan the QR code or visit DixieGillaspie.com/TTAW-Resources